Metamorphosize Enterprise IT

or

DoomIT

Rao Gudipudi

TABLE OF CONTENTS

Coming back full circle 5

Ignition Point 11

Changing Landscape of Business 59

Changing People 85

Metamorphize Enterprise IT 98

Coming back full circle

Twenty-Five years ago, just out of college, we joined companies in their IT department foreseeing a great future. At that time, a huge debate was raging among the computer professionals whether Unix systems and client/server computing would lead to the death of mainframe computers. Universities had network news and Listservs, that a few companies had access to. Worldwide Web was still the domain of discussions. Memory was extremely expensive, and we were continuously recommended to use it judiciously. Superiority of Dot-matrix printers was based on the speed of printing. Laser Printers were few and expensive, and slow. Apple computers were in the decline and at best were good for typing proposals. The news in the corridors was of a company in Seattle (of all the places) has just launched a windows based personal computer. Everybody talked about it, but nobody has seen it!

For a generation that worked on both Unix Systems and Mainframe, we were promptly put on either mainframe or client-server projects. We were amazed at the type of code written by the predecessors and longevity of those applications. There was no documentation and had generations of code in multiple versions. Half the code was not even called in the programs, and most of the active code was rarely used as they were written to manage the numerous exceptional cases. We gleefully added more lines of code and commented out the old code without removing it.

It was the time when project management was under the microscopic lenses of management due to multiple project failures. The focus was on work breakdown structure to ensure the time-cycle per deliverable was reduced in every cycle. The maximum time between deliverables was two months, and our managers constantly asked for monthly deliverables. We were forced to attend training programs on project management and writing efficient code that was maintainable and dependable. And we were doing our best to follow our seniors' footsteps in violating every one of them!

It was also the time when the business world was changing with globalization, and business process re-engineering. All the client facing business processes started changing the way they ran. The immediate pressure was felt on the IT Department as the systems were more attuned to the existing structure and needed massive restructuring to meet the changing business requirements. Process orientation of applications instead of department orientation became the buzzword.

As we were wading through this potpourri of complex computing technologies and contributing our two cents to the debates on client-server versus mainframe, jokes at the coffee machine started that the head of the department was looking for somebody to investigate on something called year 2000 problem. Quite a few people were offered and turned down as the problem looked preposterous and it was more than eons away. We were more concerned about the happy hour on Friday than something that was 6 years away. We were absolutely convinced that whatever we wrote would be replaced in the next 5 years, either by recent technologies like ERP or pure obsolescence.

Imagine our surprise, when we were called into a meeting one day and told that we are responsible for getting the company ready for Year 2000! More than the problem being handed to us, without choice, we were more worried about becoming the target of endless jokes in the department and at the coffee machine!

The source was an article in a *ComputerWorld* magazine, with a heading DOOMSDAY! that said if you are not prepared for Year 2000 all the companies that used computers would cease to be in business.

We started looking at every major maintenance article in both public and scientific journals, including the Journal of Software Maintenance, and found nothing. How do we oversee something that we do not know where to look for, and above all what to look for? As young people who were used to using the system date, our immediate assumption was that is CTO problem and systems need to upload a patch or something and we can all go back to our normal work life.

But we had a manager who believed in a detailed report with every t's crossed and i's dotted. The rumor was that the manager was the first person to join the company when we called as EDP department. He knew every application, and every line of code. Our first option, to provide a quick report, that put the problem squarely at the CTO table flew away.

We started talking to the various managers, and IT professionals. We got more hints over endless cups of coffee than in the formal meetings. Formal meetings were primarily to tell us that there was no problem. It was over coffee, some sympathetic colleagues started telling us all the nightmarish scenarios of the predecessors coding with no coding standards, no documentation, no test cases, and packed code.

We got our lucky break during a conversation when we received two credible starting points

- Most of the code in the system is not even called during any of the application processing and they have not seen them being called in the past few years
- In the early days, date was just a variable, and that one of the early programmers had named it after his pet!

It was the second point that intrigued us the most, as we already had some clues on the first, but not the size. We started looking at the earliest code in our domains and imagine our surprise when we realized the earliest programmers used a six-digit variable for date and had called it under different names, based on logic. While reading the code, we had to relook at the functional logic to identify which of the six-digit variables were date-fields and which were business variables. The problem multiplied as the predecessors renamed the field at will. The date fields were named after their pets, mothers name, children name, favorite characters, and any other word except being called a date!

This episode started one the biggest change management process in the complete IT Industry. It may be the last time an enterprise looked at its complete application portfolio.

At the end of Year 2000, the whole episode has been written off as scare mongering by IT Professionals and in some cases were even ridiculed. Many people who worked on Year 2000 programs have either moved to management or moved out of their respective technology domains to newer technology pastures. Many removed their expertise in managing year 2000 programs from their profiles, and quite a few renamed them as maintenance projects to avoid answering the sceptic questions on year 2000.

The result of all this is the paradoxical situation that the IT Departments are currently placed in today. Unless we launch another enterprise change management to redefine the scope of IT and its role in enterprise business, we are looking at DOOMSDAY! for many businesses. The issues are emerging in sporadic cases but have not become a full-blown enterprise issue. If there is time to act it is now!

Over the past 25 years, I have interacted with hundreds of developers and operations team, both as program manager and operations manager observing at close quarters the magnitude of the issue. With the challenges and issues faced during Year 2000, it gives me a special perspective on what we are foreseeing. Beyond this I have also engaged in discussions with many colleagues at various events and friends who have moved on to newer technologies. Many have become reluctant to discuss Year 2000 or draw parallels with Year 2000, but every time they speak, I have nagging feeling that they are discussing the same issues as in Year 2000 and hinting at enterprise change management is very much due. In the very least, many of the learnings of Year 2000 change management have been duly forgotten, leading to a more complex situation.

Ignition Point

It is imperative to set the context to the ignition point that we currently find ourselves in. Most of the IT departments have evolved from the erstwhile EDP departments of the past. These were primarily processing data with rudimentary analysis and reporting capabilities that enabled companies to store enormous amounts of data. In the early days of computing kilobytes of data was large data, and EDP departments were off bounds to business users and only a select few had access to computers.

As EDP departments evolved into IT Departments, and companies started on the computerization drive, investing in terminals enabling business departments to use computers for their operations. The IT departments started computerizing the as-is process of each department. With the cost of memory being a premium, the programmers had to ensure that every byte of memory was used optimally. The paradigms of programming were efficiency, and packed code not leaving a single byte be wasted. The cost of memory ensured that money cannot be wasted on comments and other documentation. Documentation was maintained in volumes of hard-bound books or thick folders, and rarely referred or updated.

Besides the programming impact, the applications were written to reflect the business structure in existence at that time. The computer systems only replicated the organizational structure and were primarily for improving operational efficiency. During the initial stages, it was common to have department wise applications, and except for specific data flow logic, these applications had little to be connected to each other. The changes in business was static with minor changes over the years. Applications were written in these scenarios and were expected to run for few years without any changes. Maintainability was never a consideration as the assumption was that if the department structure ever changed, you just rewrote the whole program. Changes were slow and with considerable time lags defining the change management process.

With memory being extremely expensive, processing efficiency was defined by the code with little or no reliance on the processor speed. Data processing was time consuming, and summary batch reports taking a couple of days was acceptable, as this was more efficient than in the era of books, which required weeks to consolidate and had to be rechecked multiple times to ensure that they were error free.

The second benefit was that the complete data resided in one location, the computer, then in multiple books, that developed the habit of getting misplaced. The data resided in multiple spools of tape that was under the control of the IT Department. The data could be traceable by giving sufficient notice to the computer team to load the data spool tape for a specific time period.

A few enterprising IT Departments went a little ahead and tried to automate the business process by adding logic to their programs.

Companies started adding additional logic program flows for doing some advance calculations like ratio's, balance sheets, and consolidation of regional sales.

As time progressed, more logical reasoning was built into the programs. The logical reasoning that was purely dependent on the experience of the senior manager slowly started moving to computer programs, providing better data inputs to the senior managers to support in decision making. Decision making models were rare, and very few. IT was never a differentiator nor was considered as a business enabler. It was purely an operational system to improve efficiency. IT enabled the departments to substantially reduce the time of operational requirements. But all process and controls from the past were retained even in the computerized era. The management of each department had all the aces, that were held closely as decision-making process rested solely with them.

But one rule defined all programming. Business was static and if the business ever changed, they will rewrite the complete program. Mergers and acquisitions were fewer and merger activities used to take their own time to integrate the systems.

As the enterprise structure rarely changed, IT department never felt the need to rewrite their applications and they developed processes and procedures that would define on running the same programs and applications in the new operating systems or version changes.

Managing version changes with the least effort was the rule of the day, and IT Departments spend in improving their efficiencies in managing version control, when it occurred. The operating systems and languages used to have an upgraded version every few years. As the newer versions were fully backward compatible, enterprises rarely felt the rush to upgrade to newer versions. Hardware providers continued to provide support to older versions of operating systems, tools, and language compilers even after newer versions were released.

Waves of Changes

Into this era of quite bliss, the first wave of changes started occurring, as companies started facing business disruption. With global trade, the established companies started facing low-cost alternatives from around the world. Companies were forced to take out costs from existing operations for survivability. IT provided the perfect tool for pushing additional cost cutting.

Enterprises started using global procurement and manufacturing to maintain competitive advantage. To track these globally distributed procurement and manufacturing, IT became the core integrator of all the disparate locations facilitated by improvements in communication infrastructure. Online communications and wide area networks using satellite communications enabled the data to be transferred from one location to another without delay. A combination of rapid progress and the drop-in prices in communication led to massive adoption of computers across the globe. The benefits of having information available overnight far-outweighed the costs of communications and computing. Companies could look at reducing costs of inventory using just-in-time processes and relook at the complete procurement and manufacturing processes.

At the same time, enterprises started looking at their internal process, and realized that by standardization and centralization they could remove redundant and duplicate jobs. Best practices of delivering more with fewer resources became the norm leading to massive restructuring of internal departments like accounting, procurement, invoicing, payments, and recruitment, led by ever increasing IT presence.

IT departments also felt the same pressures impacting the other departments to deliver more for less. As the pressure on IT department started to deliver solutions that would meet the businesses cost-out initiatives, IT Departments instead of rewriting the applications started developing interfaces to ensure that the applications spoke to each other. This ensured that IT Departments met their objectives, but at the same time, applications that were written more than a decade or two earlier got a fresh lease of life. The basic assumption that the programs will be rewritten for organizational changes was completely forgotten.

During this surge for change, old programs were commented out or interfaces developed to ensure that data flows through the program without any processing. Substantial number of application programs residing on systems as IT Departments forgot to remove them or cleanse the systems of old programs. The other assumption was that these applications may be useful in future when there are other enterprise changes. The programmers assumed that instead of rewriting the whole application again they can use the existing program to meet future changes. Enterprise systems started accumulating massive amounts of dead or unused code. This usually led to slower response rate and excessive usage of computing time, leading to bottlenecks.

It was also the time when IT started facing a huge backlog of maintenance and change requests, with more than 80% of maintenance and change requests going unanswered. The change requests were never answered on demand and scheduled in queue. By the time the change request was taken up the business requirements have changed leading to IT questioning the maintenance and change requests. This led to process definition requiring multiple approvals, and further delay, but with a difference, instead of IT being the cause of delay, it is now the process. The process also helped in creating an audit trail on the source of change request, approvers and the time taken to implement the change request. The process also enabled IT to weed out on-the-spur requests from business users and enabled the IT department to focus on genuine business change requests. But the effect of this was that business users anticipated delays from IT.

To improve the efficiency of IT Systems, many companies started on rewriting or reengineering the applications. The biggest challenge for these projects was all the backlog of maintenance and change requests for bundled with the reengineering/rewriting projects leading to frequent changes, with a fancy name, scope creep. This led to innumerable delays and projects exceeding their budgets and failure was more common than success. Except for small projects any large projects were doomed and assumed to be a failure. Failure being defined as not delivered, or not delivered to specifications, or not delivered on schedule or delivered with delays and cost over-runs. One of side-effects was that the original source code was commented out and was left to reside within the system without being deleted. Due to the multiple interfaces that were developed over the years, some other applications might be calling the original application for specific functionality leading to the original applications never being retired or removed from system. Compounding the problem for retiring applications was the lack of documentation that never detailed the applications that were interfacing with original application. And due to compartmentalization of applications based on enterprise departments, the interface would be controlled by another application manager with the current application manager having little or no clue.

The situation was at best chaotic and managers were happy managing the current application by patching up and writing piece-meal code to keep the application running instead of looking at the bigger picture.

At the same time, to overcome the delays from IT Departments, business managers started looking for alternatives that they can develop locally within the department without alarming the centralized departments. They started developing client-server and desktop applications that they can use locally within their department with little or no connectivity to the centralized IT Systems. Most of these are client focused or with specific departmental requirements to meet the business demands. The cost of these applications was negligible that business managers could manage within their budgets. As these applications started becoming critical to meet the business needs, and hold critical customer data, these applications were interfaced for data exchange with the central IT departments. These applications again were plagued with the same challenges as early systems like no documentation, user developed for specific requirement, no functional requirements, and no maintenance. It was the norm for each of this client-server and desktops having the multiple versions of the same applications. Sometimes developed by the same person at separate times or by multiple persons. Sometimes the whole application was developed from scratch instead of modifying an existing application even for minor changes. Some of these applications were developed by dedicated IT professionals working within the business unit, but more often, an IT Savvy business user wrote the code on the fly with no standards or documentation. As the business user changed his role, these applications became orphaned.

As these business unit applications started becoming critical and large, the control of these applications led to friction between business units and IT Departments. This led to multiple command and control issues between business users and IT departments. Where the business unit gave up control or vice-versa it was done with lot of skepticism and questions. In many cases, these applications were just abandoned with business users and no management control either by the IT Department or business department.

The Rumpus

Into this rumpus, a new breed of IT vendors started gaining entry to the IT departments and business. The early vendors focused on code generators and other programming tasks. The new breed of vendors came with applications that can meet a complete departmental requirement like accounting, human resources, payroll processing etc., As these application packages started maturing, they started adding other functionalities to their core application to become enterprise-wide application packages. Based on their original core application many of them gained entry to enterprise IT through their respective business units.

Many enterprises started implementing these packaged applications with customizations to meet their specific business requirements. But the core concept remained that they were specific to a business unit and had interfaces to other applications from other business units. The stove-pipe structure of the application development age continued to the package application age.

It was not uncommon for enterprise to purchase only one module of the enterprise application (usually the core application package) and this model became popular as "best of breed" solutions. Enterprises used to source financials from Oracle, HR from PeopleSoft, Production and Materials Management from SAP, and CRM from Seibel, and integrated them. To enable this competitive model, enterprise applications integrators provided the middleware for all these disparate applications to speak to each other. What started as a solution to rid of legacy applications, the logic was transferred to the new system, making them comparable to legacy applications even before they were implemented. This was led by the rigid approach of business units in identifying their application package. The IT department was left with integrating these multiple application packages at the data layer or application layer to enable these applications to speak to each other.

As the best solution for enterprise transformation was raging in the companies, the discussions on Year 2000 started increasingly being discussed and the doomsday scenario started playing in multiple versions. Consultants, Vendors, and Press started discussing the Year 2000 issue with little or no actual anecdotes. All examples of IT failures including bugs, abends et al became a year 2000 issue. Even bad programing that led to errors were blamed on Year 2000. And as the doomsday predictions became increasingly virulent, the scope of Year 2000 started expanding. From a complete lack of data, Year 2000 teams in many companies were getting flooded with examples of how Year 2000 would impact the enterprise and more often they were too far-fetched. Many of these articles started talking as if the complete enterprise will get locked out, and employees may face challenges in entering.

What started as a pure application programming issue started becoming a monster with multiple tentacles. Even some of the systems which were beyond the control of internal IT Departments were getting flooded with requests to validate for Year 2000. Even systems that have nothing to do with date fields were also being pushed to IT Departments for validation. The articles started talking of ubiquitous presence of IT inside the enterprise and added to the confusion. Remote articles by experts started appearing about air-conditioning getting switched off, process controllers failing, doors getting locked out, escalators and elevators getting stuck. Doomsday scenarios were being written about even for normal routines and functions that have absolutely nothing to do with date processing.

The biggest challenge for these types of projects was the starting point. It becomes extremely difficult even to pinpoint the problem. So, we took a stepwise approach to the challenges at hand.

Step 1: Identify the number of programs and lines of code. This rudimentary problem became a major challenge as we did not have a clue on the number of lines of code or number of application programs. The normal rule of thumb from multiple customer interactions was between 2 to 3 times the initial estimate. For one client, we started with the client estimate of 6 million lines of code and when we did a complete inventory, we found 22 million lines of code. Luckily, there were people who had actually worked, written or made some changes, in those programs and they could help us locate the missing programs. Many of them were completely surprised that the program is still being called, as they had assumed that the program has been retired. There were stray incidents, where we did face challenges in locating the source code on the main systems, as most of the inventory of applications was being done in batches in individual servers and desktops.

Step 2: Identify all the languages, tools, and databases. More often than not we identified language code or tool generated code that the client had no clue they existed as they have stopped paying for the maintenance and slowly these just dropped out of attention. Some of the language providers and code generators were no longer available for getting clarifications. As most of the data was saved in flat files identifying the datafiles was a relatively easier task. But the challenge was the columns or data fields had no documentation attached and the current employees were not even aware of why that data was collected.

Step 3: Mapping all the programs and interfaces. This was an easier said than done even with robust tools available. Primarily due to security concerns, running any tools on the mainframe usually met with a security brick wall. With minimal capabilities of servers and desktops, trying to map all the programs in batches was a major concern. Identifying all the places a change at one place may have an impact and the interfaces was a nightmare. Sometimes a variable is introduced in an application program and is not called anywhere else for any type of calculation. Sometimes a variable may be called for multiple times from multiple programs. It was also common for active programs to call for a program that has been completely commented, or to utilize only a few lines in the hundreds of lines of code.

Step 4: Identifying the date fields. With a complete lack of coding standards and date being a six-digit variable unlike current systems that clearly identify the data fields, this was a humongous challenge. The early programmers called the date field, by any name of their choice including their pet names. In multiple scenarios, these variables were renamed, and some with no apparent reason, except for the fancy of the programmer. But, in multiple places, these were renamed with a specific purpose and utility. The date field (six-digit variable) was processed through multiple conditional coding with no functional relevance and was used at multiple places.

Step 5: Prioritizing. This proved a huge challenge as the application managers of the critical programs were skeptical. To prove the viability, we had to start with peripheral programs and slowly move to the critical core applications, but it was also imperative that we did not back-end these critical programs to ensure that all changes to these programs had sufficient testing time and post-production run-cycles. All programs were categorized into the following: Non-critical applications for initial changes, critical applications, critical core applications, non-critical programs for later changes primarily desk top programs and stand-alone applications. Also, we relied that vendors would release year 2000 compliant code and patches to their existing application programs. This was especially true for desktop applications and embedded systems. Most of the doomsday predictions were actually concentrating on the last part, i.e., vendor dependent applications that the internal IT Departments of enterprises has little or no control and cannot make any changes.

Step 6: Solutioning. Though everybody started discussing that Year 2000 should be corrected and the solution seems to be clearly visible, the ground realities proved to be challenging. The best solution would be just modifying all the six-digit date fields to eight-digit date fields by adding the century to the year. But this proved more of a mirage than reality. Due to this the more frequent solution was Windowing or its variation sliding window using any combination of 80/20, 60/40 etc., This solution involved added a few lines to the application on interpreting the six-digit variable. The other major challenge posed during the solutioning phase was the maintenance work that was conducted in production to be included in the modified applications. Many were easy to do, but it was not uncommon that in some cases it ended literally redoing the whole work again.

Step 7: Testing. Though every company has enough test cases, they are never enough. Also, many companies never assessed their data based on dates. Dates as part of other testing that calculate periods of time were available. But the test cases never included when dates themselves were to be tested. Test scripts were rewritten. The other biggest challenge was to ensure that date changes did not affect any other logic. At the same time, the change requests that were incorporated along with date changes were also managed and were tested to ensure that the application worked as it should be and did not have any side-effects.

Step 8: Moving to Production. This may be one of the few times that application software code was being moved in such a large scale from test environment to production. Millions of lines of code were being moved out of production and was being moved back in.

Beyond all this, Year 2000 Projects taught a lot to enterprise IT Departments

- ➢ A complete inventory of all applications including the applications in central systems and departmental systems along with specific relevant information like language, tools, and interfaces,
- ➢ Ability to focus on the core issues and not get swayed by the buzz created
- ➢ Managers and programmer's knowledge about enterprise-wide large-scale change requests

- Change Managers who can manage to remove from production, modify, manage, and put it into production of live applications with little or no interruption of the daily operations
- Ability to develop utilities and tools that automated the repetitive processes that could be used across applications
- Learning to prioritize based on business and IT requirements, and ensure that the plans defined were adhered to and delivered as per plan
- Creating a central library of date routines that that can be used by multiple application programs

Besides all the positives, the year 2000 projects also caused disruptions to businesses

- New technology adoption like WWW was delayed as the companies were focusing their budgets on Year 2000 project
- maintenance and business change requests were put on hold leading to an increase in backlog
- Rewriting or reengineering of applications was pushed back and Year 2000 changes took top priority and the budgets were consumed in Year 2000 remediation
- Application life was extended as companies had spent substantial budgets on year 2000 remediation and were in a rush to catch-up on pending maintenance and change requests

One of the causalities of the budgets being diverted to Year 2000 projects, was the Computer-aided software engineering tools that was heavily discussed before the Year 2000 projects started were put on the backburner. They took another half-a decade before they could be launched again but with different features. The original CASE tools that were code-generators lost out, but tools for modeling, designing, and testing survived, and thrived.

The loss of CASE tools is still being reverberating across the industry as the original software productivity tools lost out in the race. Just for illustration, the author was selected for a training program on a code generator tool for Java, that started spreading for all Web based applications. One of the examples illustrated was building a simple mathematical calculator. I took four hours to develop the calculator using the Java code generator. After the training program, during a discussion, the benefits of the code generators came up. One of the project managers was not keen on the code generators, and when I explained that I took four hours to develop the calculator and requested her if she can put her best programmer to develop the same without code generators. After about a month, I received a call from the project manager, requesting me to meet her. During the meeting she said that she had put the challenge to all her team members and to track the time. The team members took anywhere between thirty-two to fifty-six productive hours. She introduced me to the team and then I introduced to the concepts of CASE Tools. We had a detailed discussion. But for all its productivity enhancing capabilities, the downside of CASE tools (code generators) was that they created a lot more number of lines of source code compared to directly writing the source code. In some cases, as many as 7 times the number of lines of source code. In an era when processor speed, and memory was still a premium, the additional lines of code complicated the response rates. Maybe, if these had survived, over a period of time they may have become more efficient and better in managing the source code.

It was also during this time that many companies transitioned out of legacy applications to newer packaged based solutions like ERP etc., The only challenge with this transition was that even though companies started implementing package based solutions, legacy code was kept in abeyance for an eventuality, and in many cases still resides today. Many of these package-based solutions still were an extension of the earlier stove-piped departments or replicated the same structure under a different name. Enterprises were reluctant to change from their existing structure. IT was being viewed as competitive differentiator and not as a cost and efficiency center. This put the heads of IT Departments under tremendous pressure to perform and try chart into different territories that were the domain of the business managers. With the departmental applications reverting to central IT Departments during the Year 2000 and migration to packaged solutions/ERP, the control horizon and the assets under management went up exponentially, but with little or no increase in the budgets of IT Departments.

For all the buzz of doomsday and frenzy, the Year 2000 passed peacefully with no impact and new year was welcomed with all its celebrations. Nobody was stuck in lifts. No HVAC system stopped working. Nobody got locked out of their system. The people who worked on Year 2000 projects faced ridicule and were mocked for wasting companies' precious resources (people, budgets, and time) on a mirage. As the spectacular failures failed to materialize, many people started questioning the Year 2000 issue itself. Just like in the pre-Year 2000 days, stories of failure scenarios were being written, post- Year 2000 comments started appearing, especially in online forums like blogs, questioning the Year 2000 issue itself. There were a few stray incidents that actually occurred, but they occurred a few months after Year 2000 cross-over and were buried in the multitude of other articles.

The Winds of Change

As the enterprises were struggling with Year 2000 problem either by remediation of the data changes, or replacing with Packaged solutions, the world was being overwhelmed by the world wide web. The roots that lay in the defense sector and was extensively used in the universities among students for communication and chatting suddenly became available to all. The early internet was primarily a communication tool used for email, listserv, and network news (nn). Even in those days, it was not uncommon for listserv or nn getting flooded with messages. As the business and IT professionals used to using computers in schools and usage of computer to computer communication started joining the workforce, they started changing the basic nature of internal IT systems and those frustrated went out to start a wave of internet age companies.

Due to the time-lag for established companies to join the web or online world, a plethora of online companies started forming. Online Banks, retailers, insurance companies became the flavor with little or no physical infrastructure with deep discount pricing models. This has led to massive market disruptions to the established hierarchy of business. With no physical boundaries and the barriers of globalization being torn down, these companies became global from day one of their business. These companies were not relying on established communication protocols but were using computer to computer communication or data communication for establishing and growing their business. Aiding and supporting these enterprises was tools like Netscape, Yahoo, Lycos, etc., that provided a global marketing platform.

As the established enterprises were still debating on how to exploit the internet, security of data, and the competitive differentiation they have due to internal IT Systems, these companies were openly embracing the new technology and put their complete company information on the web for consumers to read and interact with them. Many of these companies leveraged the internet to test the scope of their marketplace and the boundaries of the governmental regulation. Government regulation was trying to catch-up with the speed of changes, then actually regulating them. Governmental regulation hindered the established enterprises in looking beyond and openly embrace the innovative technologies.

The new-age companies embraced open source the ubiquitous term used for all free software. They started developing on open source technologies and customize them for their internal requirements. They developed their own architecture and started releasing their architectural notes for public domain. They openly discussed their software, and applications. They would give back to the community by releasing their internal applications to open source community. They completely redefined the way applications were being developed. They leveraged the applications developed and released into open source community for their internal application development. For any applications they internally developed they released it into the community for testing, and for developing additional features. Their testing and additional development costs reduced as they adapted the works of others and released their code back into open source community. Due to the reduced costs of application development and maintenance, these companies could focus on their core business area and leverage the complete open source community as an extension of their IT Departments. These companies rarely saw their applications as a competitive differentiator, but how they use them to provide the competitive advantage. This also provided them to experiment and develop new technologies internally and release the same back into open source community for adoption. As the open source community started developing additional features, these companies had their choice of features available to them at no cost. These companies were eager to adapt and use any innovative technology within their frameworks to ensure that they can provide a unique experience to their customers. As the world-wide-web started exploding, these companies started feeding more information to the consumers and maturing into online retailers, banks, and insurers.

At the same time, enterprises that believed that their IT systems was their competitive advantage, build firewalls and were slow to adapt to the new technology. Even when they adapted innovative technology of internet and web, they were cautious to start with providing only the basic information. Even manuals that are usually in public domain, when a consumer buys their product, was considered as propriety, and was not made available on the web. Enterprises build additional processes to identify and acknowledge, and to some extent certify, what information can be made publicly available on the web. To facilitate these additional layers additional applications were written. With the early architecture models that depended on rigid compartmentalization, trying to get information at a central source became a challenge. As enterprises started changing, they were hindered by the age-old architecture models that were never changed. To overcome these challenges, a plethora of integrations solutions under the common vocabulary of Enterprise Application Integration Tools were implemented. These provided integration at data-level, and application level. The only advantage these applications provided was providing a layer above the existing applications to enable them to talk to each other. It was not uncommon that some companies used multiple integration applications leading to these integration applications themselves becoming their own core sub-department within IT. These applications had little or no additional business value except to make applications speak to each other.

Dichotomy of Core Systems

As the technology landscape changed from web information to online transactions and onward to mobile technologies, Enterprises started using intermediate layers to enable these applications to be web-enabled or mobile friendly.

As multiple middle layers were being created, and the availability of resources in traditional technologies started dwindling, enterprises started writing more business logic code above these layers in newer technologies. Even the technology landscape changed to enable enterprises to start working with the middle layer instead of working on the legacy applications. Tools and integration applications were available to bridge the legacy applications and new technologies especially in web and mobile spaces. These further enabled enterprises to move their development and maintenance away from the legacy applications to the new applications that were being developed and maintenance above the integration layers. With passing time, these newer applications became the go-to systems for maintenance, with little or no maintenance or updates being performed on the legacy applications. The large amount of source code in legacy applications was wither forgotten or rarely maintained. A decade ago, it was estimated that legacy applications accounted for 80% of all source code. Even adjusting for correction factor due to changes in computing environment, it is still a huge chunk of source code!

Enterprises that had moved to packaged applications like ERP etc., were using integration applications to provide best-of-breed solutions. As enterprises started picking the various modules in packaged applications, enterprise application integration solutions played the critical role of integrating these independent modules into a cohesive application. These enterprise application integrators enabled the core applications for web or mobile as the technology landscape kept changing.

The other major advantage these application integrators provided was a common interface across applications enabling companies to use reporting tools. This ensured the enterprises to reduce the licensing costs by providing a reporting layer and giving access to the reports. With user licensing fees for these packaged applications being high, enterprises were always looking at reducing costs. The cost of the integration applications and reporting layer software was by far cheaper than taking additional licenses of the core packaged applications. Using a reporting layer enabled the IT departments provide enterprise reporting at a fraction of the cost and was able to change or reorganize the reports without lesser effort and costs than trying to make any application changes. Even today, it is common for business users to use an independent reporting layer like PowerBI or tableau instead of the reporting capabilities in core CRM or ERP due to cost differential.

These Enterprise application integrators enabled companies to move from stove-piped architecture applications to integrated applications. Enabled the companies to adapt to changing organizational structure without modifying the underlying applications. Using these middle layer applications enabled enterprises to move online and mobile enable their applications without the costs of rewriting the core applications and meet the market demand.

This mode of transitioning of applications by using middle-layers has become the norm including moving the applications to the cloud and mobile. Enterprises have started investing in the higher layers than on the core layers of technologies.

Even today, core application processing happens in the legacy or traditional systems. But these applications are rarely maintained and only upgraded to run in newer version compilers with minimal or no changes to the applications. Robust test cases have been developed to check if the systems are working properly after any version change.

These middle layers ensured that legacy applications, written over 50 years ago, are still running. Besides extending the life of legacy applications, they provided other benefits for many IT Departments. As newer technologies came like Java, Python, .NET etc., the available resource pool for legacy applications started shrinking. Many of the early programmers had retired. The programmers during Year 2000 had either moved out of legacy technologies to newer technologies or moved out into other roles.

As per a series of articles in Computerworld and other magazines that appeared about a decade ago on the fiftieth anniversary of COBOL, we had a million COBOL programmers, i.e., approximately 7% of the total software developer professionals in the world, maintaining 80% of the code. That raises series questions that 93% of the software professionals were working on 20% of the software code, and probably on new development. The other fascinating fact was the average age of COBOL Programmer was 45 Years, whereas for most of the other newer technologies the programmers were in the mid to low twenties. If we progress the data and extrapolate it, even though the software programmer pool may have grown exponentially in the last decade, the growth is primarily in the newer technologies. The absolute number of COBOL Programmers would have shrunk compared to 10 years ago. And if we progress the average age of COBOL Programmer, it may be beyond 50 years now, and many of the senior people at the top of the curve may have retired or contemplating retirement, shrinking the COBOL Programmer pool even more. Even going by conservative estimates, the COBOL Programmer pool may have shrunk by 15 to 20% over the last decade. This pool will continue to shrink. Most of these COBOL programmers would have joined during the Year 2000 projects have an inkling into the various programs. They have the experience to look for missing or dead programs that are in the systems. The other challenge as the legacy applications programmers may have also moved out of these technologies and moved on to newer technologies in search of greener pastures.

At the same time, the number of applications that were rewritten or reengineered or rearchitected have not been consistent with the changes in the talent space. Enterprises started leveraging the middle layers to go beyond basic integration to overcome this imbalance among resource availability. Enterprises also started doing absolute minimum with the resources available and getting the development and maintenance work being done in the middle layers or popularly called as wrappers. The author in discussions with various colleagues realized that maintenance project team members rarely or never look at the code in the core application. All their application maintenance activities are performed in the middle layers.

These middle layers also facilitated in massive cost cutting measures across the enterprise. As the process orientation was facilitated by IT, many of the business functions could be split into core business functions and back-office operations allowing the business leaders to focus on business growth, and back office operations be managed by other managers. As the back-office operations started growing, enterprises started tracking the workload and realized that by sharing resources they could try to reduce the number of people in the back-office and optimize the resource allocations and costs. The back-office operations that were part of business functions slowly evolved into shared service centers that had their own reporting hierarchy independent of the business functions. The units within the shared service centers had a dual reporting line to both the business functions and shared services center managers. This slowly evolved into more process driven than becoming flexible to the changing business needs. Change management became a full-fledged function. Unlike the earlier days when business functions could reorganize to the business needs, the new structure ensured that proper planning and scheduling has to be done to perform the change management. The change management process is rigidly defined that by the time change is approved the business requirements have changed.

During the Year 2000 project days, service providers have stepped up to support in the enterprise efforts to complete year 2000 projects. Year 2000 has led to large projects being moved to offshore locations around the world like India, China, and other low-cost locations. This has led to 24-hour delivery cycles taking advantage of the time zone differences between the locations. As the service providers at these low-cost locations were hungry for business, they were glad to take the Year 2000 project. Many of these Year 2000 projects metamorphized into maintenance projects for legacy applications. Enterprises were eager to leverage these low-cost locations for maintenance works and release their budgets for development projects in web and mobile. Over a period of time, enterprises started moving more work to these low-cost locations as the budget squeeze due to cost cutting measures forced them to look for cheaper alternatives.

It was at the same time, shared service centers started discussing of moving to low cost centers to move their back-end business operations. The service providers in these low-cost locations proceeded to provide 24/7 support and agreed to work in customer time zones. Enterprises started moving work to low-cost locations, and the distance between the business functions and the back-end operations started widening. Customer call centers the first line of communication with customers was moved to low-cost centers. As time went by the client facing operations like call centers, and help desk were moved out of the enterprise to service providers in low-cost centers. Customer feedback which used to be first line of information for business functions has now become a cost center and moved out to service providers. Other Shared Service Center operations like Finance and accounting, billing, desktop support, internal support like help desks, were all moved to service centers. The Shared service centers of service providers provided higher accuracy and speed compared to internal shared service center in many cases leading to lower costs of operations.

As the cost of operations from low-cost locations by finance were factored in, cost take-outs started looking at extending the shared services centers to IT for maintenance and development of projects. Cost takeout was extended to other development projects including web and mobile development projects. A distinct shift from non-core applications and operations at low-cost centers moved to movement of even core applications and critical operations to meet the cost reduction targets. Many enterprises, who were uncomfortable to work with service providers or due to risk management, established their own captives in these low-cost countries.

The financial crisis of 2008 led to many companies to focus more on cost take-outs. Companies realized that moving to service providers reduced their management overheads at captives and exited their captives. This led to a second surge in both IT and operations works being moved to low-cost locations around the world. Additional Low-cost locations in Mexico, South-east Asia, and Eastern Europe added to the choices of enterprises beyond the established low-cost locations of India, China, and Philippines. As the number of low-cost locations increased, enterprises were looking for best location for services and operations. In all this transformation, IT and communications played pivotal roles for supporting the enterprises in their cost take-out journeys.

Benchmarks and Consultants

Benchmark studies comparing captive centers to outsourced services gave a key metric for enterprises to look at reducing costs. It was in this process, benchmark studies started appearing that defied logic.

In one study, ERP Application maintenance, Implementation, Legacy Application Development and Maintenance, Web Application Development and Maintenance, Mobile application development all carried the same pyramid that was heavy with lower experience people. When we asked the consulting firm if the application criticality, business functionality or complexity was considered, the answer was in the negative and they categorically stated that they do not have any materialistic impact on the composition of teams. The consultants went on to explain to me as the program manager on the models to improve the team pyramid structure. Adding to this, was the continuous reference to reduce costs and adopt the models of shared services being performed in the business processes to look for leverage points to reduce the costs. The challenge with many of the consultants is they provide multiple example to tell us why and what we are doing is wrong, leading to a tricky situation that you will end up getting these benchmark metrics as your KPI's based on generalities without specific insights based on your current IT Systems. Also, unlike earlier, many of these studies are performed on assumed key indicators that usually ignores other key performance parameters making these studies irrelevant or highly improbable to implement. After this study was presented, I spoke to my manager and asked him on how he had accepted this study. Along with the manager was the Program Leader for this study. Both gave me a hard look and gave a big grin, and simply stated, if you are having this problem, imagine us. Both were actually perplexed, when I informed them that they had accepted, and we were asked to implement it. After a few moments of thought, the Program Leader remembered that in a leadership meeting a few days back, it was point number 34 that was presented and none of them had any clue. You can imagine the chaos for the rest of the hour as we all started discussing on what to do.

In another study a process improvement team focused on work force management studied the business process and reverted to me stating that we can reduce the team size by 10% based on their work force analytics study they had performed. The challenge was that they completely ignored the restrictions placed by the risk team in access controls and sharing of process among individuals, criticality of the process, the response times, and the peak volume considerations. They observed the data during a specific period when a few processes were having peak volumes and the others were not. For all the team that was not in peak volume period the consultants observed that we can share resources. The consultants had already presented to the management and had been asked to present to me for implementation. The process managers in the interim were contacting me on a daily basis with their cup of woes. I was stuck in the middle knowing what the management would expect and knowing that implementing the changes required would be next to impossible with all the risk controls, response times, peak volumes, and other factors. I started preparing for the meeting by starting to review the standard operating procedures that have been accepted by the process improvement group, risk control teams and management. I can thank my stars that day, as the meeting ended in confusion due to multiple issues with standard operating procedures and risk controls. The risk control team and process control teams who were attending the call immediately raised a major flag as the recommendations were in violations of the risk control procedures. The discussions ended without any result.

In another instance, we used to follow a simple principle of mapping all projects in the program on specific criteria in red, green, yellow format. If any project appears in red for more two weeks, we in the program management were anticipated to look into the issue and work towards early resolution. We were also expected to review its impact on the overall program. The tool was effective, simple, and manageable as we were tracking at any point between 1500 to 1800 projects across the program. The tool was defined for simplicity without loss of any critical parameters, and it was automated for approvals and consolidation. The tool enabled the project managers to spend less than 10 to 15 minutes in normal circumstances and 30 minutes for special situations, especially when the projects were in red for more than two weeks. One day we received a project tracking tool from the consultant teams, that tracked on double the parameters, and on a numeric scale with a complex instruction. This was completely in excel without any automatic consolidation requiring manual efforts and consolidation. After consolidation, based on the score, the projects are deemed green, yellow or red. After spending half a day, including a webinar, by the consultants to understand the new report, I forwarded it to my manager. He spent more than 30 minutes to understand the report and called me to explain it to him. I spent 30 minutes explaining the report, and absolutely confused him. We started discussing on the merits and demerits of the current and the proposed new report. The new report provides a quantifiable justification for the project status, but the numbers that were used for all the calculations were still based on the subjective discretion of the manager. The discretion to make a status of an individual attribute is not justified by numeric number that itself is based on subjective discretion instead of the managers discretion for directly rating it green, yellow or red. This actually may lead to other challenges by making a critical project be green instead of being red in the earlier report due to the law of averages playing at the overall report, even when we do weighted averages. Each project at the various stages of software development lifecycle will have different criticalities, weights, and challenges. In the earlier report, the project manager had the decision to make the overall project status red, based on criticality. Though this does lead to over reporting of red projects, this also ensured that we did not miss any critical project being reported green. This ensured that the program management office was tracking the red projects judiciously, and ensuring the program was on schedule with little or no delays at the overall program level. We decided to shelve the new report due to its complexity and the cost of changing the established process for over 150 project managers.

The above examples are not to say that consultants do not help the enterprise they provide a unique insight based on interactions with multiple companies. They will have access to data knowledge from hundreds of companies and insights developed from them. There have also been instances where consultants have enabled us to improve our internal processes. Some of the benchmarking studies also helped us to relook at the parameters of working environments to see if we can effectively improve our internal benchmarks and cost-takeout's. The challenge for many of us in the implementation teams would be doing an in-depth analysis of the benchmark studies as the consultants try to force a "one size fits all" studies and expect us to deliver to their benchmark studies and not as per your environments. The other challenge with these benchmarking companies is their attempts to standardize on IT projects and business processes and try to common benchmarks. Invariably these benchmarking studies are for reducing costs and less on effective execution of projects and meeting SLA's.

During all this, over the past twenty-five years, another department went for a major transformation. The Quality Assurance department. What started as an internal model for ensuring high quality without interfering in the managerial decision making, and as an enabler to improve the managerial decision-making process, has slowly evolved into every aspect of managerial functioning. And in the process, it has lost its edge as a decision enabler to a paper process.

It is not uncommon for many projects in red to actually receive commendations from the Quality Assurance team only to find that the project is facing multiple challenges during the development lifecycle or during the implementation phase. The managers instead of looking at the real ground level situation and resolve it are prone to review their quality process documents to identify the issues. Adding to the woes is that instead of having quality process team consisting of experienced people in that area, many of them have grown within the quality assurance team with little or no practical software development knowledge. They rely more on paperwork, checklists, and artefacts. Projects would get sterling reports on the quality process followed by a specific project but continue to have severe developmental and execution challenges. One of the first things, we had to do, was delink the quality process from project status reporting to ensure that we get a more accurate picture of the status of the multiple projects we were tracking.

In these twenty-five years, as we moved from managerial decision making to process driven, the number of processes or procedures defined for a manager has also increased multi-fold. This has ensured that many managers instead of relying on their expertise and experience to decide are relying more on the process. The biggest casualty of all this, the intuition factor, that led to many managers effectiveness using his experience and expertise to take a decision is now rarely visible as the managers increasingly rely on the process.

When I interact with my colleagues or speak to my team members, their first response to think outside-the-box is their inherent fear of breaking any of the process or quality procedures. They have been ingrained from their joining date is to follow the process and procedures with enough examples on how different projects have succeeded by following the defined processes and procedures., As most of these presentations are usually done by people who are rarely associated with the project, they cannot provide the insights from the project except the matter in the notes sections or speaking points that are documented in the presentation. There is now an inherent fear to take a decision outside the processes and procedures defined due to the indoctrination the team receives at the time of joining and the reinforcements through continuous emails and additional training modules.

The irrelevance of these training programs can be best explained by one standard example that most of us would have heard in multiple training programs. Most corporate trainers use this as an example, a person is walking down a road and sees three workers. He asked the first worker what he was doing, the worker answers that he is laying bricks. He asks the second worker; the worker responds that he is building a wall. He asks the third worker and his answer that he is building a cathedral. The tragedy of this example is these trainers can't even make one minor change and apply it to the region or audience and state that the third worker replies as building a church, temple or mosque or any other building other than a cathedral.

The other challenge that does not equip the team members by these process definitions groups and quality assurance groups is the examples provided during the training programs. The examples are too simplistic compared to the real problems being faced on the floor. Same or similar examples are used for new recruits and for mid and senior managers. The least these managers can adapt is based on the experience profile of the audience to change the complexity of their examples and use relevant examples.

Complicating the issue with Quality Assurance and Process groups is the constant fear of Risk Controls and Audit Teams. The impact of Quality Assurance and Process Group, Risk Management and Audit has increased exponentially over the last two decades making independent decision making a challenge. Many managers have resigned to the factor that it is better to follow the process and procedures than to challenge the status quo even when their own intuition is strongly advising to look at an alternative.

The other casualty is diversity of opinion. Earlier any planning session or review session used to be lively with extensive debates with both the pros and cons being discussed. All meetings used to be in a meeting room with all the relevant members being present. All members were encouraged to prepare in advance and come with alternative solutions or counter points for the agenda. If any presentations are made, they were usually handwritten on OHP slides or even if using a computer, the presentations used to be simple with 4 or 5 points per slide. The presenter needs to have a good proficiency in the subject with less points on the slides and content delivered was high. This ensured that the attendees listened to the presenter and ask questions based on what the presenter spoke. The discussions used to revolve on presentations made. Though sometimes these debates used to prolong, there was always a sense of respect among the members of the meeting that usually led to the maintenance of decorum. The number of meetings were fewer and even if a meeting ran overschedule, we used to focus on completing the agenda without deferring. This invariably ensured that the best solution after in-depth discussion of both the advantages of disadvantages of the project used to be taken forward. Invariably one of the members would suggest a really "out of the box" solution. More often than not the solution that evolves would be far simpler than the original proposed solution. These diversified opinions used to be encouraged and discussed. But today, these opinions are rejected or frowned upon as they do not follow the defined processes and procedures. Any deviation from the defined process and procedures would lead to audit and risk management questions.

Today meetings are encouraged for more of dissemination and gain concurrence, with little or no discussions being encouraged. Any counter point or alternative solution is usually stated for offline discussion, or in general parlance the point can be dropped, and no further discussion will take place. Also, there are days when senior and middle management are rushing form one meeting to another and their preparation for the meeting happens during the meeting. Due to the number of meetings, most of them are online. Though this encourages larger audience, it also leads to the question, if all the members are really required. And during the meeting, how many of the people are actually needed for the meeting. It is no wonder that more than 50% of the meetings that middle and senior managers attend have no relevance and these people would be shaking their head on why they were invited for the meeting itself. As the presenter usually reads the slides, the audience would have read the slides and rarely or never listen to the presenter. These sessions sound more like the early TV comedy shows that are recorded in front of live audience, who are usually prompted for laughter and clapping their hands. Just like these early TV Shows, the audience for these presentations clap at periodic intervals. It is not uncommon for presenters to request their colleagues to ask a couple of questions to ensure that will not provide an opportunity to any embarrassing questions. In the process, all efforts are made to not encourage any alternative thoughts and let anybody ask a counter-intuitive question that may have led to a more robust solutioning.

In all this, the biggest bogey man shown is the Audit and Risk management teams. Any alternative question would receive a response that the process does not allow that, or we need to discuss it with risk management team. After a few such meetings, the audience gets to be finetuned to start their webinar session and continue to do other work instead of concentrating on the meeting. So technically if 50% of the audience for the presentation are wondering why they have been invited or questioning the relevance for them to attend the meeting, and another 25% has already switched off due to non-encouragement in earlier meetings, and the balance would be discouraged by showing the bogey of audit teams, risk management teams, processes and procedures.

In this process, one of the tragic cases is employee engagement. There was a time when senior management used to engage with all their team members including team members who were 4 to 5 hierarchical steps below them and could be seen talking to them. This used to be a big morale booster to the junior level employees and was a bragging point among the juniors. Due to the number of meetings todays senior management is expected to attend, they have little or no time to engage with their junior employees. To address enterprises has put this as one of the KRA's for senior management and the solution is a townhall. So technically they are meeting without actually developing any insights into the team they have. Their only assessment of their teams is through the daily, weekly, monthly reports they evaluate. In the eagerness to break the hierarchical structures, we have also increased the distance between the senior management and the employees for reasons that may not be directly attributable to flat structures.

The perfect ignition mix

Over the last twenty-five years, business changes and IT changes have been following each other's or in leading each other. For Example, business process reengineering led to a massive integration of IT systems. Globalization and Web technologies moved hand-in-hand. Web, Mobile and other online technologies have led to a fundamental shift in the way we do business and we interact with the customers.

In all these changes, one key parameter that played was cost reduction or improving efficiency. This has led to a focus on costs by all established organizations moving away from growth focus to cost focus. As growth focus was led by new enterprises, established enterprises focused on cost reduction. Even in highly regulated fields the focus was on cost reduction. Even the stock markets focused on cost effectiveness and cost take-outs than on new avenues of growth.

The brick and mortars business obituary was written even before the online business actually made profit. The question would be if the obituaries written led to the acceleration of downfall of these businesses. Even when the online businesses did not make profit and were bleeding money, they were rated highly, and established enterprises showed even a small dip in their profit due to business cycles their obituary was written. In the process, we have effectively muddled up the multi-channels for customer experience. Over the past couple of years, when we tried to buy online or through a brick-and-mortars business, the price differential is extremely low for most of the items like books, and mobiles. There have been occasions when the price at the nearby store had a better price than an online store.

As a frequent flyer, another industry that completely confused me was the airline industry. During the 90's when the airline industry entered turbulence, every airline was compared to a low-cost carrier and benchmark studies done for reduction of costs. Till then I never travelled in the low-cost carrier and was frequent traveler in one of the major airlines. The biggest reason was for a frequent traveler like me, having a relaxed meal that served on the major airlines was a life saver, as I used to literally run between meetings to airports. Even on short duration flights of one hour or so, adding the journey time from home to airport and journey to client place, the duration spend on the flight was the only time we could afford a relaxed meal. There are days when the only meals were those that were served on the flight. When the benchmark studies started punching holes in established airlines, the airlines started cancelling out on the meals. Today we do not differentiate between major airlines or low-cost airlines, and the passengers are forced to pick their own meals from the airport. That has removed the reasons for flying major airlines. Also, it has added to the woes of passengers as they go through the additional security checks and add a few minutes they need to stand in queue to pick up their meals before boarding a flight. The meals that used to cost a miniscule fraction of flight ticket ended up becoming the biggest casualty of the airline industry. This has led to passenger also becoming more flexible in travelling in any airline instead of the airline of choice. The only saver for loyalty to an airline is the frequent flier program. It will not be surprising at the next instance of turbulence analysts will start reporting that frequent flier programs are bleeding the companies and advising airlines to dump the frequent flier programs or start reducing the costs of frequent flier programs. There are frequent flier programs that are dictated by the price of the ticket and not just the miles of journey.

In both the cases the primary reason for change was cost reduction, and customer became second. Enterprises that used to run with customer experience as the central pivot for all their activities slowly moved away from customer at the core to cost effectiveness. They started leveraging technologies like voice response systems, automated customer calling systems, auto checking etc., under the guise of increasing customer experiences and reducing their waiting periods. But the fundamental concept of customer experience that can only be obtained by personal interaction has been distanced. This removed the differences between online models and traditional models. Due to this both online business and traditional business started losing their qualitative perspective of customer experiences. These individual experiences have now been replaced with data models that look for buying patterns.

The data models can only provide the quantitative data information but rarely provide the qualitative or emotional connect information. Some years back, a friend of mine requested me to pick up infant food for the puppies that his dog has recently given birth. As the mother feeding all the puppies was not sufficient to meet the litters requirements, my friend was feeding infant food as supplementary diet to the puppies. I was a frequent visitor to the store, and I had never bought anything that provided any inkling that I was having a baby in the house. Imagine my surprise when the cash counter printed out a coupon for diapers! Instead of relying purely on an automatic coupon, if the system relied slightly more on my discussion with the cash counter lady, they would have received the insight that I was picking up the infant food for puppies of a friend. I and the lady at the cash counter had a good laugh and I walked out of the store. At any time both quantitative and qualitative data play a significant role in customer satisfaction.

Similarly, I am used to visiting a small bookstore. The owner used to engage in small talk on slow days. It was during these small talks he used to recommend to me a wide range of diverse types of books. I was amazed at the way the bookstore owner could recommend to me various books that I would normally would not have bought. The same experience in an online store would be, based on my previous searches, they would recommend similar type of books. I was glad that the book shop owner was present to introduce and recommend various books.

A similar experience was when I wanted to buy books for my daughter just entering her teen years. If we search online, there a pre-defined set of books or teen-romance books. When I visited a bookstore, the manager of the store immediately recommended the same genre of books. I informed the manager that she has read the sets of books he was recommending. For the teen-romance, I asked the manager if they are appropriate for a father to give to a daughter. He fumbled and then introduced me to one of his frequent customers and requested his customer to help me. The moment I explained my dilemma the customer immediately took out a bunch of books and informed that the books she had picked would be of interest. All the books she picked were not in the list of books that were recommended on the online stores, and the titles themselves were odd. But when I read the back page and browsed, the books looked interesting, and I ended up picking the books. These illustrations are only to prove that to make intelligent decisions, we need both quantitative and qualitative analysis.

The above examples are to prove that there are factors that go beyond data, and that is the customer experience. IT has been the fallback medium for all these cost reduction efforts. In the process, enterprises have introduced more technologies that have been moving them away from the customer. The most important customer feedback tool for many customers used to be the customer call center or help lines. These were slowly moved to pre-defined responses using standard operating procedures, and then outsourced and later moved to an inanimate automatic response system like interactive voice response systems. These can respond to a query but rarely engage with the customer in an intelligent discussion to gain insights about the customer. They also rarely gauge the emotion of the caller, which an online person can gauge and recalibrate his answer. It has facilitated this process to meet the organizational goals of cost reduction.

As IT Departments were under constant pressure to reduce costs of doing business, they were playing catch-up with enterprise goals of cost reduction. Enterprise growth using IT as a key differentiator slowly became a casualty. IT departments continuously strived to reduce costs by leverage the existing IT assets by using multiple layers of tools to enable legacy applications for web and mobile technologies. They build layers of intermediate and front-end applications with little modifications to the back-end applications.

At the same time, even the IT departments were under huge pressure to reduce their costs, and they started relying on outsourcing to low cost locations more. It is no longer a surprise that there are applications that are completely outsourced and maintained by vendors with nobody on the client side being aware of the application, except as a line item in the list of applications in the statement of work. Many of these applications are legacy and enterprise IT departments are more focused on the top layers of the applications. After many years of moving applications to vendors and low-cost locations, the finance department has become accustomed to the cost leverages and they have now started requesting for more cost reduction both within the IT department but also leveraging IT to reduce costs across the enterprise.

As most of the companies are already working from low cost locations and with wage rise in these low-cost locations, there is constant pressure being built-up between the customer and the vendors or between the enterprise and its captives. The IT department that has been used to reduce costs for the enterprise business divisions have been under pressure for some time to reduce their own costs. During the second wave of cost reduction by the IT Departments they have been able to do so by putting pressure on their captives or vendors to reduce costs. Now, as we enter the third wave of cost reduction by IT Departments, there are huge challenges that IT departments need to address to even look at annual cost reduction.

Many of the IT departments are straddling over 50 years of applications that have been developed over multiple periods. Many IT departments have 5 to 6 generations of IT applications residing in their enterprise, with little or no knowledge of the earliest applications. The knowledge gained during the Year 2000 Projects on the inventory of applications has not been updated to reflect the changes over the past 20 years. In many aspects the situation has become regressive with early applications hiding behind multiple layers of integration applications.

With the mainframe applications programmers becoming fewer by the year due to retirement or technology changes, in the next decade many companies would have seen the last of the legacy applications programmer leaving the company carrying the complete knowledge of the applications behind the layers. These legacy applications have been completely outsourced to service providers that the enterprise has no knowledge of these applications. Enterprises have forced application programmers to work on legacy applications to bridge the skills shortage for 2 to 3 years before being moved to other IT projects. These programmers may have picked up the technology skills to maintain the applications but would rarely acquire the nuances of the complete application including its functional knowledge, and history of the application.

Service providers have started retrenching the legacy application managers under their own cost reduction measures. Invariably a number of managers that are being reduced are in legacy technologies. Service Providers across the globe who could rise up to the occasion for Year 2000 to support enterprises would find it difficult as they keep reducing the legacy application managers. Service Providers are training these managers in digital technologies and a few for completely different roles moving further away from legacy technologies. It has become a norm for service providers to use a different scale for legacy applications managers compared to digital technologies for all aspects of employee relations including wages, and benefits.

I was part of a meeting on a financial application. When we explained our capabilities one manager was skeptical about our knowledge. During lunch time, I started discussing with him. His nonchalant answer was that only he knows the application, and nobody knows about it as he wrote it and he is maintaining it. All his knowledge was in his brain. He was in no mood to share his application knowledge nor was he willing to document the application. He was used to replying that he will do it when he has the time, as he has huge backlog of requests. After a couple of years, I got the news that the person has quit. Now nobody wants to touch it nor look into the application as there was no documentation, and it was written in a legacy language, and the application was only upgraded to run in newer versions with most of code being difficult to understand. The variables also were defined as per the whims of the earlier person. There were no coding standards followed and absolutely no comments, except the old code that he had commented out. The new team just built an interface to other applications defining only the inputs and knowing what the output will be. Over a few years, they have only been adding more customizations to the interfaces and never touched the original source code. In the interim a couple of managers have changed and they have an application that is revered and literally worshipped as they have no idea when that application will fail, nor do they have any knowledge of the application. They have no knowledge to even replace the application as they do not know the business rules residing in the application.

And with continuous cost pressures that have been running the application managers are hoping that it will not fail as long they are the managers and moving on. This familiar scenario with small variations is replicated in most of the companies.

As Enterprises have lost knowledge of applications, and Service Providers reducing their staff, there are applications that are currently in no-man's land. With neither the enterprise nor the service provider having any knowledge about those applications. Their only knowledge of these application is what goes in, and what comes out.

Changing Landscape of Business

Over the last twenty-five years, the business has become more globalized. Companies that were focused on regional and national level have become globalized either in their sales channels or their supply chains. Companies that may be local from market and sales perspectives have global supply chains, with many of the parts and components coming from low cost countries. As companies become price-competitive, they were forced to reduce the costs of manufacturing by outsourcing the parts and components manufacturing. Enterprises became integrators than manufacturers. Many more outsourced even the integration and became only R&D, and sales & marketing organizations.

Even service companies like financial and Insurance companies outsourced their backend operations, IT management and infrastructure support to global sourcing vendors to reduce costs. Even the customer touchpoints like loan recovery, sales, telemarketing, and claims were all outsourced to global providers. Telemarketing became the buzz word across all the enterprises from being a specialized niche seller.

The advent of the web, and as telecommunication companies increased the speed of connectivity and cost of communication rapidly dropped, many companies leveraged IT to move to global sourcing models to reduce costs.

Due to reduction of costs, companies started seeing higher margins and were able to meet the expectations of the stock-markets and shareholders. Over a period, as companies got used to the benefits and finance started looking for more cost reductions, more work was moved to low cost locations. In the early phases, the work moved to low-cost locations was either non-critical work or low-end maintenance work. These supplemented their internal IT Staff and were primarily positioned to move only work for which they were no available skills. This ensured that most of the employees in non-critical work being moved to other critical projects, and employees who have left the enterprise, were replaced with resources from low cost locations after internal movement of available resources to critical projects. This enabled the enterprises to meet their requirement of skilled resources in legacy technologies and at the same time reduce their costs. Year 2000 Project heralded a higher movement of work to low cost locations as enterprises could not find enough resources in legacy technologies in the local market and the cost-benefits played a major critical role.

After the Year 2000 Project phase, work started moving to low cost locations in two major streams. Both having critical shortage of skills. One was the legacy applications that need to be maintained. And the second, that had a shortage of skills was Web technology skills. The legacy projects that moved to low costs locations were maintenance type of activities with no major development effort. Most of the development was in the web technologies, but in the initial phases, web development was primarily associated with content management and little or no transactional applications being developed. This ensured companies to announce their web presence and provide as little as possible except for a few enterprises that embraced the new technology.

As the web applications started becoming more complex with transactional applications being developed or being interfaced to legacy applications, enterprises continued to move work to low cost locations. As the complexity of the applications and capability of resources increased, more work started moving to low cost locations. During this process, even client facing applications and operations were moved to low cost locations.

A similar trend in manufacturing and industrial products also occurred leveraging the advances in IT and communications, companies could manage their global procurement cycle. This enabled them to keep the procurement costs low, reduce their inventory cycles and improve their time to market.

Computing advances like laptop, tablets and mobiles ensured that enterprises can coordinate with their procurement and IT cycles irrespective of the time zones. Enterprises can check their procurement or project status live every day and take corrective action to ensure that their production cycles are not impacted. Enterprises could also build a network of suppliers instead of relying on sole sourcing for better management of delays or disruptions from one location or provider. As enterprises could commoditize their requirements by documenting clear specifications, they could also move from one supplier to another without major disruptions. This reduced their dependency on a single or a few vendors, enabling the enterprises to bargain for the best price.

Even IT applications moved from the domain of specific expertise to the level of a commodity driven by shared services models, and improvements in communications. This enabled the enterprises to provide flexible working models to their employees enabling them to work from anywhere in the world and still provide the same level of productivity. It is not uncommon for employees to work from remote locations for periods of time for personal and family reasons. Employees could work from home taking care of their children and adjust their work schedules around their personal schedules. Even with all this flexibility, employees could continue to deliver as per schedule and communicate with their colleagues. Collaborative tools enabled the employees to stay connected even from remote locations. This provided an additional benefit to enterprises as they can reduce their real-estate costs. From the earlier model of one seat per employee, currently companies have flexible seating models, that encourage working from home, and fewer seats at the office than the number of employees at any given location.

Enterprises started encouraging their employees and partners to use their own devices. From an era of enterprise supplied hardware and software, enterprises moved to an era of providing only the software and encouraging their employees to bring their own hardware like laptops, tablets, and mobiles. Security concerns that led to enterprises providing mobile phones and laptops to ensure secure data were removed with the advent of virtual private networks and the ability to provide a secure work environment for their employees. Bring your Own Device replaced many of the hardware-based security concerns to a more software-based solutions. Employees started having complete flexibility to use their device of their choice to work on their office work. Many of the employees were ahead of the technology curve by using the latest top of the range gadgets.

This led to a tricky situation for IT Departments. From an era of telling employees what systems they can use and what they cannot use, suddenly employees have become empowered to use their systems of choice and add-on applications. Employees started playing with other applications on their systems and requesting the IT Department to provide access to the same. The best example is the reporting systems. Employees stopped using the reporting provided by their internal IT Departments and started downloading the data into Excel or other worksheets. Employees started writing their scripts in Excel to do their own data analysis. The same is true for presentation software. It is common for employees to purchase their own add-on templates and feature-rich slides that would enhance their presentations. These software add-ons excel scripts and presentation add-ons are usually driven by employee's desire to make the best impression to their managers. As most of these software add-ons are low-cost it is not uncommon for most of them to be acquired directly instead of going through the procurement process.

These directly procured software add-ons had a low shelf life and may have been used once or twice. Rarely do these software add-ons used multiple times. After using them a couple of times, they are replaced with another software add-on to ensure that these employees always had the latest tools. More than the use of the add-on's, enterprise data started getting distributed across the enterprise. These software add-ons also enabled employees to republish their presentations with minimal changes for multiple meetings and make any changes quickly.

As mobile apps from online stores became available, employees started using them for both personal and office related work. These mobile apps extend the current capability of the enterprise applications to provide the reporting of their choice.

With frequent changes occurring in organizational structures, and the enterprise eco-system due to both regulatory and management changes, these software add-ons provided employees to repurpose their reports to the new structure with minimal or no support from their internal IT Departments.

Management reporting that used to be tedious process with multiple levels of reviews for a once-a-quarter meetings are now held more frequently. There are occasions, when we used to start preparing for a quarter-end report one month in advance collecting both the quantitative and qualitative information, putting them into a presentation deck and review at multiple levels. The only information that was updated two weeks before the meeting was the numbers. We were mandated to send the presentation to CxO office two weeks in advance. Due to the time-lag from preparation to presentation, most of the information was outdated, and risks that were identified used to be resolved or mitigated during this period. The performance review meetings usually end-up with one of the attendees stating that the issue is already resolved. From such a cycle, now both management and employees would like to see their reports being done either with that day's data and verification being done online. It is common for management to check their online system for the latest data as presentations are being done by the line managers.

Shortening Planning cycles

During the early 80's and 90's, enterprises used to draw multi-year plans. It was not uncommon to hear of 3-year, 5 year and 10-year plans for enterprises. Enterprises used to spend substantial time to review their long-term strategic plans and plan for the changes that need to be done within the organization to meet these goals. An elaborate training plan used to be written and change management process was given its due credence. The same model was followed in IT application development and strategy. It was not uncommon for IT Departments to prepare their long-term strategy and work towards implementing it.

As enterprises started globalizing their procurement and production processes, IT departments were under pressure to meet the requirements of the business. The scope of an IT department suddenly increased from managing their internal IT Systems to coordinate with multiple supplier systems and trying to integrate to their internal systems. As the vendors had their own home-grown systems, integration of these systems posed bigger challenges.

The ability to frequently change their vendors or the flexibility required to integrate new suppliers and vendors, made the IT departments to shorten their planning processes. At the same time, with advent of technologies like tablets, and mobiles, IT Departments were trying to enable their existing applications to be accessible on the new devices.

Due to the frequent technology landscape changes, IT Departments started looking at commercially available off the shelf products and presentation, most of the information was outdated, and risks that were identified used to be resolved or mitigated during this period. The performance review meetings usually end-up with one of the attendees stating that the issue is already resolved. From such a cycle, now both management and employees would like to see their reports being done either with that day's data and verification being done online. It is common for management to check their online system for the latest data as presentations are being done by the line managers.

Shortening Planning cycles

During the early 80's and 90's, enterprises used to draw multi-year plans. It was not uncommon to hear of 3-year, 5 year and 10-year plans for enterprises. Enterprises used to spend substantial time to review their long-term strategic plans and plan for the changes that need to be done within the organization to meet these goals. An elaborate training plan used to be written and change management process was given its due credence. The same model was followed in IT application development and strategy. It was not uncommon for IT Departments to prepare their long-term strategy and work towards implementing it.

As enterprises started globalizing their procurement and production processes, IT departments were under pressure to meet the requirements of the business. The scope of an IT department suddenly increased from managing their internal IT Systems to coordinate with multiple supplier systems and trying to integrate to their internal systems. As the vendors had their own home-grown systems, integration of these systems posed bigger challenges.

The ability to frequently change their vendors or the flexibility required to integrate new suppliers and vendors, made the IT departments to shorten their planning processes. At the same time, with advent of technologies like tablets, and mobiles, IT Departments were trying to enable their existing applications to be accessible on the new devices.

Due to the frequent technology landscape changes, IT Departments started looking at commercially available off the shelf products and customize them to meet their internal requirements. In the early phases, IT departments used to lead their innovation and launch new applications that would put them in the forefront of business and enable in making substantial business changes to the way enterprises operate. Over the last two decades, IT Departments are playing catch-up with technology, and more often than not, they are looking at outside vendors providing them with the advantage over competition. Instead of being innovators, the enterprises were either early or late adopters of technology based on their internal management appetite for new technologies. Adding to the confusion is plethora of approvals that every new idea needs to go through an approval process before adoption.

As the enterprise IT department was trying to play catch-up with the changing landscape, the management was aggressively pushing for cost reductions and business units were demanding more online business enablers to be ahead of the competition. As the IT Department got stuck between these two conflicting requirements, instead of spending on research and innovation, the IT Departments started focusing on adopting newer technologies using outside tools with minimal modifications to the existing application infrastructure.

Though the hardware was constantly getting upgraded with the latest processors, memory and storage devices, application infrastructure was rarely upgraded or rearchitected. The backbone of enterprise IT Departments, the enterprise architecture group slowly shifted from launching new business solutions to provide new technology interfaces to existing applications. New Application Development has been redefined to be more of an integration of applications and enabling the existing applications to newer devices.

As if to fill this gap, service providers started working with enterprises on different pricing models of engagement besides the traditional time and material development. Service providers started providing fixed price, transaction-based pricing, and other pricing models. For common applications like finance and accounting, claims processing etc., service providers launched platform-based business process models with a transaction-based pricing model. The only challenge with all these pricing models were the basis for computation still revolved around the number of people working on the project. Any attempt to delink the pricing from headcount was usually not feasible due to the service providers internal systems or were not appreciated by the client's management. In one client project, a service provider won the project on transaction-based pricing with a clear inbuilt pricing model that up to 10% of additional volumes would be managed within the current budgets. The project manager realized that he could do a series of technology interventions by which he could reduce the headcount on the project. One of the process involved a team to take the data from one system and input it into another system. This usually led to multiple errors as sometimes the amount used to be entered in invoice number field and vice versa leading to small amount payments suddenly showing as a multi-million-dollar payment. There used to be an additional team that used to check for these errors. The Manager decided to develop an interface that would automatically populate the fields from one system to another. Thereby he also increased the speed of transactions, improved the accuracy from 95% to 99%, and reduce the headcount. Within two years of starting the project the project manager reduced the headcount by half, and at the same time exceeded all his SLA's.

During the mid-contract review, the customer could renegotiate a higher SLA and were being achieved. During this period, a customer representative visited the service provider and realized that only half the team was working. He was totally confounded on how the service provider was able to provide higher accuracy and meet his higher SLA's though he could not achieve it for more than a decade. On his return, he initiated internal discussions on possibly moving it inhouse, and finally after a year, the customer decided to establish his own low-cost center and moved the project inhouse. The project manager left the service provider after a few days as he had lost a customer. But in the complete process, innovation suffered both due to lack of sight by the service provider and customer. The customer had signed for transaction-based pricing model and could successfully negotiate higher SLA's leading to higher customer satisfaction, and the essence of platform-based business processes was for service providers to provide automated solutions thereby reducing headcount and improve his profitability. After a few years, when I met the project manager and enquired, he was happy doing time and material projects and looked at me with disdain if he was still doing any technology interventions to improve the process. Now, he is only looking at improving the headcount and do "just enough" technology improvement to meet his SLA's.

The other biggest challenge for service providers to provide cost effectiveness is the reluctance of enterprises to allow service providers n sharing resources. One key benefit of working with service providers is they can share the resources with multiple customers based on the peak cycles of these customers, in a shared services model, and meet the SLA's. But in reality, resource sharing rarely happens even though the model of engagement would be based on SLA's, the data will revolve around headcount.

During this time, cost reduction irrespective of the market scenario became the norm. During slow periods, cost reduction was used to meet the profitability targets. During the other times, cost reduction was still continued in anticipation of market slowdown in the future or based on performance of peers. This has led to an apprehension among employees on trying to meet only the stated goals instead of trying to exceed the percentage of reduction anticipated. Due to the constant pressure of cost reduction, people have started innovation by force instead of by enthusiasm. Unlike the earlier periods, when innovation in IT was encouraged by the business teams as enabling them in their daily job, the innovation in the past couple of decades has primarily focused on cost reduction. Though there have been cases of innovation in IT and Operations Groups, but it has been under market or peer pressure. The best example is the enterprises move to online (web or mobile) was usually driven extensively by market analysts, investment analysts, and new competitors that were completely online.

During the same time, the legal and risk compliance has become more complex for managers. Managers who used to focus on running and growing the business have to start looking for all the legal and risk aspects before deciding. During the last part of last century, managers used to make the decision and send the decision to legal and HR for confirmation or comments. But in the current environment, these decisions are being pushed to business managers through educational programs like training or eLearning, and enterprises expect that the business managers ensure compliance as per risk and legal requirements. As the laws become more complex, the enterprises are forced to move it to business managers, and business managers role has changed from running and growing business to include understanding HR, Legal and Risk.

This has led to a unique situation, where existing enterprises were measured on performance and profitability and any difference in a point in the expectation was reflected in the stock markets. At the same time, the new online enterprises were measured completely on a different scale of potential growth instead of profitability or performance. With the online enterprises promoting price gaps based on the business model they propounded, analysts aggressively propagated established enterprises to move online to reduce their brick-and mortar structures. As the online enterprises start becoming large market euphoria is over, it has become quite normal to observe that the price advantage has narrowed.

The changes in these two decades have ensured that all established enterprises have seen their core business models changing to embrace online business model. And the online businesses establishing brick and mortar structure. This has led to all enterprises becoming a mixed business models, thereby removing any price advantage. For many of the items available through online stores, the actual price paid by consumer is comparable to the price in a brick-and-mortar store.

As the Enterprise IT department concentrates on cost reduction or technology enablement of existing applications like moving online, business managers are forced to look beyond for applications for business enablement or business growth. Business managers have started looking for point applications that would enable them to grow their business or to meet customer experience. With the advent of "stores" by enterprise applications, business managers are leveraging these applications from stores to enhance their experience. The best example of this model is that most of the Client Relationship Management Software (CRM) have extensive stores that provide enhanced reporting capabilities. Most of these CRM come with rudimentary reporting capabilities with limitation to the number of reports, options or type of reports, business managers are forced to look into the stores for additional report format. One of the reasons for the business managers looking for additional enhancements is the complex licensing structure that are extremely rigid for the applications. When the enterprise licensing rules hinder the flexibility in slicing and dicing the data to meet the business requirements, the business managers have either taken the data for reporting offline or used the application extension available in the stores for enhancing their reporting capabilities.

Innovation and R&D

As the pressure for cost reduction increased, one of the biggest casualties was the in-house innovation. Many of the case studies that we read about the various innovative products from various enterprises slowly started dissipating especially in the IT Departments. The IT Departments were under constant pressure from two fronts – reducing costs and playing catch-up with recent technologies.

As IT departments constantly focused on reducing costs internally, they slowly distanced themselves from actual customers. From a department that provided business benefits, IT Departments started focusing more on cost reduction.

As IT Departments started becoming risk averse due to multiple levels of approvals and organizational dynamics to extend the business, the IT Departments found it easier to show cost reduction than innovate. Innovation usually has a higher rate of failure, and if they try to adopt an innovative technology, the probability of the new technology or application itself surviving a few years is in doubt. The IT Managers need to bet on the technology and assume that the technology will survive the initial hype. Due to the vagaries of technology survivability, most of the enterprises usually follow the late adoption cycle after the initial hype is over and they adopt the surviving technologies.

Due to this late adoption cycle, enterprise IT Department is usually laggard in technology adaptability, leading to business units taking the risk of adapting innovative technologies. The most common issue that we face in enterprise IT is that most of the enterprises clearly state that IE is official standard for web interface, and invariably we rarely see many people using it. They users would have already migrated to Chrome or Firefox. And as these are free software, these are usually allowed to be downloaded on the user machines.

Besides the basic browser, the enterprise applications still mandate that applications should be compatible with browsers that are 4 or 5 versions behind. This automatically restricts the application capabilities as the application is unable to utilize the later features of the browsers. And in many cases, the applications that were written a few years ago are not even updated to leverage the new features.

This has opened a field to new companies to leverage the time lag for enterprises to adopt to gain market share. One example that highlights this late adoption is the money transfer costs in the banking industry. In the early part of the millennium, money transfer was through checks or through money transfer companies. Even after online money transfer was enabled in traditional banks, the fees for transfer remained high due to higher transfer costs involved as banks were relying on traditional processes and technology that only removed the human interface from the bank but retained the same cost structure of from the legacy processes and technology. Into this gap, multiple online money transfer companies that provide the same money transfer facilities at a fraction of the cost have grown. Recently when my colleagues wanted to transfer money, we found the newer money transfer facility was costing us less than 10% of a traditional bank. The same is true for online payment charges facility from the new payment applications compared to traditional payment systems. Now we have an excess of online payment gateway companies with online stores and other portals offering their own payment systems besides pureplay payment companies.

Blockchain has revolutionized the way transactions are being performed and will be performed. Though it started in the world of cryptocurrencies, blockchain has now expanded into other areas of applications like procurement processes, contract management and others. This has led to a unique situation for enterprise IT systems to rearchitect their complete processes and thereby reduce the cost of transaction. But instead it has been "attached" to the internal systems. All external processes are managed by blockchain, but a version of the complete process is also maintained in the internal systems following the traditional model. During discussions with colleagues, we have heard multiple reasons like risk management, legal and audit. In all these cases, the end-user was frustrated with the number of systems he needs to approve a single purchase order or for approving an invoice.

Even a simple timesheet has become a cumbersome task as employees end up filling multiple time sheets. Employees have a swipe card, a timesheet that needs to be filled for project, a timesheet for finance to processes their hourly payment, and a timesheet that is generated by the security token based on proximity to the system. Invariably these are independent systems and rarely are they integrated leading to the hilarity of managers trying to reconcile the multiple time capturing systems and explain the differences. It is not uncommon for some contract employees filling as many as four to five timesheets as they try to be compliant with both the Enterprise and their parent organizations, besides the swipe cards and proximity cards.

I participated in a project where the customer mandated that all timesheets to be entered into a time reporting system for billing. The system was a standalone system with no interface with other systems except to the financial system for transfer of billing amounts. As a manager, I was mandated to review the timesheets of all employees and approve them in the system. The customer had another internal timesheet application that was interfacing with their project management system. So naturally all my team members were filling the timesheets on the project management systems timesheets also. The service providers I was working for had their own timesheet management system for calculating the revenues. As we were mandated to work in a secure environment, the entry to workplace has two level authentications of a swipe card and biometric system. Adding to the confusion was the client project manager was completely perplexed that he had to approve timesheets in two different systems and access another system to approve the invoices we submitted. And imagine we were doing all this for Fixed Priced project that had milestone billing! So technically, all the above effort was to maintain compliance and we still need to raise an invoice in delivery of milestone that has no relation to timesheets we were submitting. And the hilarity would be heightened when we used to receive a report that used to map the timesheets to the swipe records and proximity records. The challenge with these systems was they were not integrated, and with the size of the project manually trying to enter and verify the timesheets in multiple systems was itself a huge task.

If timesheets were the simplest to explain, adding all the other systems that we were trying to use, and many of them requiring multiple inputs in different formats, leaving little or no time for managers for improvements and innovation.

The lack of innovation has reached such perplexing heights that enterprises are forcing employees to take timeout to come out with innovative thinking. Workshops are being held. War rooms are being held, focus groups are being formed. In one enterprise we actually saw a document on innovation process that included multiple approval levels and describing investment criteria. In all this, management and teams have forgotten that innovative idea does not come at specified times. In all these years, the best innovation ideas, be it completely out-of-the-box, or incremental innovation, came from team members who were soft introverts.

In an era of elevator pitches, enterprises also rely on the same elevator pitch for ideas. But the best innovators in the beginning take time to explain their thoughts, with scattered points and even have difficulty explaining themselves in front of an audience. One high sounding question is enough for them to revert to being silent. Expecting these people to make elevator pitches is impossible. Usually these people rarely speak in forums and the challenge as a manager I used to face was getting them ready and providing the ring of support when they are presenting their ideas.

Many of the entrepreneurs in the new technology space have left their organization due to inability to push their ideas within the organization. When I speak to entrepreneurs who had earlier worked in enterprises their usual answer is that they were frustrated with the number of systems that involving duplicating of information, reporting, compliance, and management overload that they decided to quit a do something on their own. Their usual answer is that instead of spending time in multiple timesheets or approving they would like to spend the time on doing more productive work related to their core job profile. Most of the people reported that they spend less than 50% of their time on their actual job profile and more time in reporting, compliance and attending meetings.

The Bane of Data

Every colleague I meet have one common crib; they are attending meetings that are increasingly confusing with the analytics that were presented in the meeting. As Enterprises collect more data both from internal sources and external sources (consultants, benchmarking studies, internet searches, database providers), the amount of analysis has exponentially increased. As gap between enterprise IT departments and business widens, the analysis being presented by enterprise IT departments and their offspring enterprise data departments moves further and further away from reality.

It has become common for enterprises look for that Eureka! moment and are trying to identify that single factor or combination of factors that will provide the view through the looking glass into the future. Every small success leads to more analysis. Most of these come with jazzy, management eye catching phrases like productivity improvement, and enhanced reporting. A few may also claim better compliance!

In this elusive search, the data analyst is trying to prove that their models are superior to the managerial decision making. To prove their point, Data Analysts are putting increased pressure on other departments to collect more data. Most of the business managers who are already burdened in achieving their stretched goals and KPI's are burdened with the additional task of collecting and reporting data on multiple parameters.

During one phase of program management, I was invited for a meeting that was to discuss on increasing productivity and enable me as a program manager to manage my teams more effectively. All Managers have a series of KPI's that include proper management metrics like effort, number of bugs reported in production testing, and above all they have a parameter on the savings they achieved from budget to actual costs for the project. The savings generated was a major contribution to the employees' bonus and was constantly monitored during project reviews. The whole discussion was on multiple parameters to monitor savings. The question that was nagging me throughout the meeting was, do we need all these parameters for monitoring savings, when the financial numbers that are generated on monthly basis can do the same. The challenge with all these additional parameters was focusing on a single parameter of monitoring savings when a successful project delivery involves multiple other parameters. Also, when I asked the team if they have considered the other factors that are involved in project delivery, they said NO, and that their scope of their project was only on monitoring and increasing savings. My questions to the team included

- What happens if the project being continuously tracked below budget (or savings) but gets delayed in deliverables?
- What happens when the project is continuously going on schedule and below budget, but has too many bugs reported during production testing?
- Shouldn't their scope of definition include only successful projects with permissible limits
- And should savings be tracked at a monthly level or at a project level?

Naturally, they could not provide the answers as they were performing the analysis on a single factor.

In another of these special projects, usually led by a consultant, a team was tasked to look at the complete process of project management. After the study that involved them speaking to multiple project managers, they made a presentation to us in the management of the suggested changes. The biggest challenge when they spoke to the project managers was, they spoke to managers managing individual single projects, and naturally large projects that involve multiple project managers that are monitored as programs were left out of the analysis. The fundamental premise that the project was the individual final block led to oversimplification of project management. When the consultants made the presentation, when we questioned the team if they considered programs or large projects, their response was that they considered 85% of the projects that were being executed. Only issue was that these 85% of the projects accounted for less than 40% of the budgets, and the 15% of the programs/projects that were not considered accounted for 60% of the budgets.

A collateral consequence of these data analysts is the reporting. A couple of years ago, I was surprised to see a slide with data in 12 columns and 20 rows. Today, due to the data analytics and team's eagerness to present all their analysis and trying to comply with many corporate mandates that presentations should be about 4 or 5 slides, team members cram about 50 slides of data analysis into these 5 slides. It is not surprise that today we see slides in font size 8!

Recently we received a deck of analysis from the data analyst team asking us to validate the data that they will be presenting to senior management in the following week. They have crammed so many data points in the 10-slide presentation that should normally be in over 50 slides. But as the data analysts team had a 10-slide limit, they squeezed everything into the 10 slides. After seeing the slides, the only thing I could remember was, "if you can read these slides, you do not need glasses." After struggling to validate the data, they were trying to present, we realized that the sums in various slides were not adding up, and we are not referring to rounding off errors. The numbers in each of the slides had different numbers. When we approached the data analysts' team on the data mismatches, we were informed that the data has already been sent to senior management, and the presentation was prepared by four different analyst teams and the presentation is only a summary of their analysis. When we questioned them on how the fundamental numbers be different in each slide, and all it will take is one senior manager to compare one slide with another to get catch the differences, the data analyst team immediately fell back and said they will revert!

As reliance on data increases, managers try to perform deep dive into the data and are eager to be equipped with multiple factors of data. More often than not, they start with a pre-defined hypothesis and try to look for variables that support that hypothesis. The teams present multiple slides in multiple angles using multiple variables correlation to prove their hypothesis. But the tragedy is the analysis ignores the multi-variate nature of real data and many of the factors ignored include qualitative factors that are rarely be captured in any defined data systems. The other fundamental rule data analysts are ignoring is that a hypothesis can be proved true or false. The data analysts need to accept that it is okay that the hypothesis has been proved false. Instead of the accepting the result, they continue to try to prove it true, producing hilarious conclusions. As the data analyst team is an independent team reporting to a central chief data officer, they rarely have a comprehensive understanding of the business factors, and even rarely understand the hilarity of their conclusions.

Of late it has become a norm for large service providers stating that they are using robots in recruitment process. I had interacted with some of the companies that provide robotic support in recruitment process, and invariably they state that their robot is robust as they have collected data from the thousands of interviews they have conducted during testing. But the challenge is these robots inherently assume that the person has communication skills. But they ignore that when recruiting globally the definition of communication skills varies. A phrase that is acceptable in one culture may actually be offensive in another culture. The nuances of language and different levels of communication skills of individuals will be ignored. Intelligent, smart, and knowledgeable people may get denied purely due to their lack of acceptable knowledge of communication skills.

The challenge is once these data collections systems and analysis enters the enterprise it becomes huge challenge to remove them, though everyone will acknowledge and accept that the data system is flawed. When newer data analytics models are introduced, these old models continue to survive with an acknowledgement that most managers do not have an inkling when their managers would ask for this data. And in many cases these analytics are performed at ridiculous levels that questions the basic fundamentals of the analytical model itself.

One of the best examples for this type of analytical model that has spread raising fundamental questions is the normalization of appraisals that is used extensively in all enterprises. Normal Data assumes that we are working large data sets. Normal distribution assumes that when we take large datasets, maximum amount of the data will be closer to the mean. But what started as a normalization of performance appraisal data at enterprise level to remove individual managers biases has now spread its tentacles. It is now more common to perform normalization at project level, position level, gender level, regional office level, skill level and every other possible level. This has led to situations when normalization is being performed at individual datasets of 4 or 5 data points. This same normalization principles are being applied for projects that are being successfully executed and for projects that are in severe doldrums. Though correction factors are stated to be applied, they rarely are clear leading to confusion. These differences would become more broadcast, as the fundamental principle of normalization at enterprise level to remove manager bias has completely been forgotten, and appraisal systems use them to meet their financial goals. Due to this in many projects, the worst performing 20% would be at higher capability than the mean of another project, but due to normalization, the mean of the second project would be provided higher increments compared to the worst performing in the first project. As these individual normal curves rarely or never meet the normal distribution criteria of large data sets, any analysis or deductions derived raise important question.

As program managers we have seen better performing people from one project being rated lower than the people from other projects who would have been categorized as worst performing purely due to normalizations. Normalizations have ensured a survival of mediocrity, and HR process ensure that this mediocracy will prosper and grow.

Another drawback of normalization is that Normal Distribution assumes continuous data, and not attributes. We have force fitted a non-continuous attributes data into Normal Distribution and assuming that the data is continuous. People and People related data is never continuous and is discrete.

HR managers acknowledge the inherent drawbacks of normalization and accept that normalization is being done at micro granular level. They also acknowledge that whenever they try to rectify, they are forced to withdraw due to the opposition from business managers. As normalization has become such a commonly accepted practice, they are being restricted to only defining the percentages of people that can be banded in various level of performance. Enterprises spend a lot time of effort in collecting, consolidating, and analyzing the data for normalization of appraisals that many enterprises cannot even think of replacing the normalization process, and keep looking for the hidden gems by drilling down more for further analysis.

Changing People

As enterprises adopt to the rapidly changing business environment, the work force has seen tremendous changes in its composition and skills. Thirty years ago, technology was the domain of students in quantitative fields. Non-quantitative fields and business school students learned computers under duress. The knowledge of computers was restricted to word processors, spreadsheets, and few other applications. They were eons ahead of their previous generations, but advance knowledge was still a restricted field.

When these teams moved into the workforce, especially in the businesses, they relied on the IT department to provide the applications support and develop any new feature. But as this generation was knowledgeable of word processors and spreadsheets, they questioned the delays in reporting and analysis. They started using their knowledge to develop their reports and performing their own analysis using spreadsheets. With their management still ignorant of computer usage they had to walk a tough line in using their computer skills and working with the IT department. As their managers relied heavily on the IT department, these teams also relied on the IT Department and used their skills to fine tune the reports generated by IT Department and adding their own analysis. If any business user was computer savvy, he became a key resource in that department as his skills were extensively used by the management to present the pros and cons of their department functioning backed by analysis and good slides.

A decade later the students entering the workforce were more computer knowledgeable, and were expert users of word processors, spreadsheets, and presentation slides. These youngsters were exposed to the new wave of computing called the world wide web, and the tools that enabled the world wide web. Many of them became experts in creating their own webpages using tools that generated HTML code. This generation was fully equipped to use any tools, and knowledge of programming. But to the deference to their seniors they still relied on their IT departments to perform any application development or modifications. These users started extensively using computers for developing their reports, performing their own analysis, and presenting them in their own format. The standard formats generated by the IT department using their reporting tools became a passé that were tolerated but rarely used. They also started using their knowledge of developing web applications using tools to develop small applications that can be used within their division or department. With an active support of their previous generation, who have now moved to middle management, started developing their applications, analysis and reports using small low-budget tools. This young force was restless and wanted to move at a higher speed that the enterprises were used to, and the large timelines requested by the IT Departments to make changes were usually subverted by developing local applications using these tools.

With the boom in the early phases of web commerce, the teams could buy tools off the web using their credit cards, download & install them and start utilizing them within the same day. The business units could subvert the lengthy process of IT department and procurement approvals and processes. They were never concerned about the total number of licenses the enterprise would need, as the procurement used to validate. These new users just purchased individual licenses for their departmental usage. As the price of these individual licenses was so low, rarely were these on the radar of procurement and business users could manage within their departmental budgets. With the rise of desktop and web tools that enabled these users to develop better analysis and present them in their viewpoint, business users' reliance on Enterprise IT drastically reduced for reporting. Centralized reporting was purely for information and compliance purposes. Every Manager wanted their teams to develop unique and visually appealing presentations that would encourage them to generate a favorable opinion. Slowly these teams became restless with the scheduling timeframes from Enterprise IT Departments and started developing their own applications to meet their requirements. And with the active support of their business managers, they started requesting for data flow from the Enterprise IT to their departmental applications. They usually looked for ways to bypass the enterprise IT to meet their business requirements, and with their fast turnaround times, usually had the support of their business managers. These business applications that started in reporting slowly started developing their logic and grew to encompass increasing business logic.

Many of the web applications and portals were launched and managed directly by the business users instead of waiting for the Enterprise IT to develop their web applications. Many enterprise web application developments usually had a major component of migration of multiple web platforms to a standardized platform. As these web applications were content driven, implementation of Web Content Management Systems and Portals became an Enterprises IT Initiative. By the time the Enterprise IT Department announced their initiative, the business units had their own web content management systems using multiple vendors.

Every year the workforce entering the enterprise from schools and universities are more IT savvy with many of them eons ahead of the enterprise IT departments and their compliance standards. They constantly challenged the enterprise IT in adapting new tools, devices, and technologies. With the rise of web tools and technologies, Open Source also started revolutionizing the way IT procurement was managed. Though it faced its band of naysayers and questions of proprietary in enterprise, Open source tools and technologies continued to develop and strengthen. Schools and Universities started adopting the open source tools as they had lower security concerns compared to Enterprises and viewed the advent of open source as way to reduce their licensing costs. The drawbacks of open source tools were managed by third party stack developers and testers who enabled individual to install open source software with minimal challenges. Even Open Source Software developers became more user friendly and strived to make their tools and technologies easily installable. During this time, open source development firms developed a dual business model of providing the base software for free and charging for support. These open source companies completely disrupted the established costing models that were primarily based on licensing and maintenance. As these individual licenses or installations were usually free, business users freely adapted them. With BYOD, these open source solutions became easier to install and manage by individual users as they were the administrators of their own devices.

During the same period, the rise of internet technology companies and web commerce with their low initial investment using open source to support their technology backbone captured an entire generation of software professionals. A multitude of startups focusing on niche areas of operations catering to a global customer base that disrupted all established business models captured a generation of employees to become entrepreneurs.

As the millennials moved from schools and universities to the workplaces, they were already computer savvy learning computer programming in schools. They had advanced skills compared to the enterprise IT departments and for them the charm of working for enterprises waned away. Most of the millennials were more interested in tech savvy companies focused on internet technologies or were interested in establishing their own startups focused on new mobile technologies. For a generation that grew on learning about the innovative technology savvy companies, their focus shifted to become the next unicorns. Facilitating the process was the new technology companies that provided most of their applications, and tools as open source. Even the proprietary software companies made their APIs available for free. The millennials started working on developing small features that were made available at a small price to existing customers and enterprises. With the advent of application stores by larger software providers that provided a marketplace for their tools, the millennials could develop and market their products and services and focus more on technology. The application stores provided these new age entrepreneurs focusing on additional features a way to reach the costumer without spending on marketing or sales.

Open Source and Mobile technologies have just erased the barrier of age for entrepreneurship. Many of these new age millennials turned entrepreneurs are not even of drinkable age. These people view any work with enterprises as a transition phase for sustenance till their applications or tools find enough users or till, they get their first round of funding. The best of the talent is more entrepreneurial than their previous generations as they passionately believe that they have the next unicorn idea that will replace all existing businesses. With the numerous layers of approvals enterprises have to approve a new idea, the millennials find it frustrating and unable to comprehend the time lag for implementation of new ideas. With the availability of open source tools and API's from proprietary software companies, the millennials believe more in developing these tools during their free time and launching their own products in these stores. As their focus is only development, with complete marketing and sales cycle including consumer feedback being managed by the larger store owners, they can leverage their technology skills in developing their products and enhance them based on the user feedback.

These Stores also enabled enterprise business users to access a talent of professionals without actually hiring them and still get the benefit of utilizing their skills. They can leverage the latest tools from market place, for enhancing their business, reporting and analysis without approaching the Enterprise IT. Business users from the millennials being IT savvy leverage these skills to integrate the software available in application stores to enhance their own businesses or support their business unit in launching new services and products.

The next generation of students entering the workforce will be even more tech savvy and entrepreneurial. They have learned or done some form of development using their mobiles. For them laptops and desktops are archaic and should be in a museum. They have learned to use the application stores extensively. Even now most of us hand over our mobiles for configuration to a teenager and they would not only do what we request but also install a plethora of bells and whistles that we would have not even heard of, and give that funny look of ancient folks for not even using them. If we see a teenager mobile, heavily personalized, and cluttered with multiple applications, each with a specific focus. They may be using WhatsApp to communicate with their parents. Instagram for their friends and another tool with their closest circle. They would be having multiple messaging tools. They are active on Facebook, twitter, and Instagram. And above all, they use their fingers to type something only in the rarest of times. They would be more used to voice based commands. More often than not, their only finger touch to the mobile is to open the security on the mobile.

When we were discussing about enabling our teams with recent technologies like Python, AI, Robotics etc., one of my colleagues remarked, that they are teaching Python in high school and that they are learning to develop robots using AI and other technologies.

A couple of years back, in a function, two millennials, one in high school and the other an undergraduate, were discussing a project involved in the development of a robot, they have done as part of their schoolwork. They had posted them online and had viewed them. The college student developed a robot with remote control on a laptop, the high school student developed a mobile controlled robot. They started discussing the way they had developed. After a few minutes, the high school student was shaking her head vigorously, and I asked her what happened. Her response was why did the undergraduate have to use basic coding when there are enough free tools from various universities available that have the same capabilities, provide higher flexibility, and reduce the effort. She was just flabbergasted that somebody would program from scratch instead of using Scratch from MIT Media Labs. And she was equally mystified why the robot should have remote controls on a laptop and not on a mobile. And these were both students with a few years gap, imagine the opinion of these youngsters about us!

The new generation that is heavily used to personalization, technology savvy will be entering the workforce. Many of them may not even have a technology background, but they are at the forefront of technology adoption. The established rules of IT security and compliance with a focus on usage of laptops and desktops will be overturned by the next generation. They will be more mobile friendly or even more comfortable using wearable computing. Established IT product companies will be old fad, and they would like to constantly experiment with recent technologies. A generation that is comfortable using multiple tools and technologies to meet their requirements. Many of the current ways of working would be archaic and frustrating for them.

We may be entering an era when business users are more tech savvy than IT professionals. A few years back, during a compliance meeting on Bring Your Own Device, the compliance manager, one of the business managers and I decided on a joint walk around our respective departments. Imagine our surprise when most of the youngsters had the latest Apple and Android phones and we the managers were using Blackberry's. We asked a few of the team members on why they do not use blackberry, their prompt response was that it was for old people. We requested their permission and asked them to show the applications they have installed on their mobiles. Most of the business users had a lot more applications, free and purchased, that they use for both their personal and business work. The business users were extremely comfortable in using all the additional applications and were enthusiastically telling us on the new cool applications that they have seen and may install it either in the evening or during the weekend. Their mobiles were heavily customized to meet their personal preferences. The variety of applications varied and covered a broad spectrum of applications.

The IT users had also downloaded the applications, but fewer applications compared to business users. Most of their applications were free and for personal use. Most of the IT users used their mobiles primarily for their personal use. The IT users used their laptop for office work and mobile for personal work.

During our next weekly meeting on compliance of BOYD, we had a lively discussion, and IT managers replicating their internal IT user profile and business users reflecting their business users' profile and the two streams rarely meet!

The other stark change in people behavior is the way research is done by these employees. Unlike the earlier generations that were used to reading large, multi-page documents and books, the next generation is used to browsing everything on the web, and anything longer than a Wikipedia page will be lost. One of the benefits of larger documents or books is the ability to present multiple angles to the same issues in detail and if possible, illustrate to make a point clear. This enables the readers to look at multiple angles and provide clarity for or against the core theme of the book. With online searches most of the illustrations or counterpoints usually become hyperlinks that may or may not be opened, leading to the reader being conditioned by only what he has read. Though the argument can be that the type of books picked up by previous generations usually conditioned them, the next generation may develop an even narrower opinion. Instead of reading multiple books to form an opinion, they would directly search for the information they are looking for and ignore the rest of the information that may lead to a narrower approach to the problems. Faced with a challenge they would just browse the internet and look for the suitable answer without trying to go through the hyperlinks.

As we move forward and the next generations start entering the work place the difference may become even more stark, with business users being at the forefront of technology adoption and IT professionals lagging behind, especially in the mobile space. The business users may have no knowledge of legacy application technologies, but they will be extremely IT Savvy. And as the enterprise IT department gets demystified of their technology halo by the IT savvy workforce the process and organizational delays may slowly lead to business units taking control of applications. Business managers with decades of listening to the delays from enterprise IT would encourage their teams to build applications on their own. The small steps most of the business divisions have taken in acquiring small tools may extend to other business areas, as they strive to achieve their business targets and KPI's.

With a plethora of online training courses and open courseware, it would become easier for the business units to encourage their teams to learn newer technologies without budgeting for their costs. Many software applications providers are already providing trainings and webinars for free to encourage their technology adoption. With Open Courseware any person can learn any technology without waiting for their organizational budgetary and managerial approvals. Many enterprises have also moved their training material online and are available for any employee to do any courseware, and employees are encouraged to do courseware from other business areas.

Employees can also use a combinations of training programs to better equip himself in the marketplace. An employee can learn about their internal Sales Process and the internal CRM using their enterprise learning portals. The same employee can also enhance his knowledge by using the CRM vendor online training programs (like the trailheads of Salesforce) to enhance his knowledge of the CRM to better give him insights into his data than the standard reports provided by the enterprise. They can also learn about Data Analysis and Visualization tools using the open courseware and perform analysis using R and develop insightful analytics using visual tools like Tableau. As most of these require an employee to learn during spare time and does not need any budgetary or managerial approvals, the employee can learn and utilize them to become more effective in his daily activities. He can also use these to make an impression with his manager by presenting insightful analysis of his performance.

Even the Enterprise training programs have changed from long-term value generation through training and mentoring to immediate cost realization. With multiple technologies and methodologies in the marketplace, enterprises are facing an uphill task to retrain their employees. The focus of the training programs has moved away from providing technology and business advantage to more immediate requirements. Immersive training programs have been replaced with eLearning. Though the benefits of eLearning are the ability to reduce the costs of training and provide access to a multitude of people, it lacks that immersive feeling that usually is experienced in a classroom environment.

Many Enterprise IT Department are forcing their employees to mandatorily undergo legacy technology training and forcing employees to spend a couple of years in legacy environment as they try to bridge the skill gap in the marketplace. Most of these employees are given a crash training program on legacy technologies and put on legacy application maintenance. These employees typically spend a couple of years of forced technology adoption and then move on to other technologies. As these people spend the time forcefully, they rarely look beyond their application or try to understand the application landscape of their company. Though this would meet the immediate enterprise requirement of skills shortage being bridged, but in the long term as multiple batches of these people rotate, the complete application landscape, its architecture, design, interfaces, and other functional knowledge of these applications would be lost. The in-depth knowledge required when multiple failures occur would not be available with these resources.

With Enterprise IT Departments looking at the mountain of legacy code they need to support, they need to constantly look back. The Business Users having no such compulsions would look forward to the latest tools and technologies in their areas of business. This constant diversified view would lead to interesting periods into the future.

Metamorphize Enterprise IT

If Enterprise IT Department needs to stay ahead of the technology curve that is enabling or hindering the business, they need to completely metamorphize themselves to make themselves relevant. If the IT Lifecycle, till now, is like a caterpillar, forming and growing devouring every leaf (cost centers in enterprises), it is time the Enterprise IT Department enters a Cocoon to transform themselves into a beautiful butterfly showing off its brilliance and ability to fly to meet the oncoming business challenges and expectations of its business users. In the process it has to go through a painful process of facing some difficult questions and take calculated risks for the future.

If the first 60 years of Enterprise IT has taught us to survive like a caterpillar, it is time, that the Enterprise IT enter a cocoon phase for preparing for the future. Enterprise IT needs to enter a cocoon phase to emerge as a beautiful butterfly ready for the next century. Enterprise IT needs to do deep thinking to decide on its role in the future of an enterprise and how it intends to make those goals achievable. Enterprise IT needs to take tough decisions and, in the process, may antagonize some of the senior management. But this insightful discussion needs to happen in every enterprise between management, business units and IT.

One key point to note is that during metamorphosis, the behavior and DNA of the caterpillar gets transferred to the butterfly. I am implying that Enterprise IT needs to metamorphize itself without losing it core behavior nor lose its DNA, that has been embedded into its applications. But these applications need to be completely metamorphized for the business requirements of the future.

During the first 30 years of Enterprise IT, there was a relative calm and stable business with long term planning and strategy. The next 30 years have shown that enterprises have to be nimble to survive, and their long-term plans became defunct by the time the planning was completed. For the future, these companies need to become even more agile and look for lightning moves from their extended competitors. The definition of competition and extended competition have been completely erased and enterprises are scrambling to define competition.

The established rules of business are getting erased as new companies enter in the gaps of existing rules and regulations and slowly expand forcing the established rules to be changed purely on the sheer size of these organizations. The principle of adhering to rules by established enterprises are constantly challenged and gaps in the armor or leveraged to the maximum.

To meet the future business requirements that are changing constantly, Enterprise IT needs to rearchitect the complete application portfolio. Instead of attempting to extend the life cycle to meet the existing business needs by using middleware and integration layers, the complete application portfolio needs to be redesigned from bottom-up.

The future model should provide complete agility to not only changing business requirements but any unseen or unexpected competition landscape that may emerge. In many cases this may also involve a complete reversal of the plans under execution. This would require enterprise architecture to be completely nimble.

Enterprises need to define their architecture with a clear anticipation that application development may no longer be in the domain of Enterprise IT but will be with the business users. Enterprise IT would only support the business departments for the core applications and all others are managed by the business users. To meet this requirement, Enterprise IT Department needs to critically evaluate "bring your own application/tool" to business users.

Though companies are projecting using DevOps and Agile to showcase that they are future ready. These efforts are like running 100 meters sprint with chains. Their majority of their applications including the core applications are in legacy technologies build decades ago. These stove piped applications have been integrated using multiple layers of middleware and adding a layer of incremental development done in DevOps or Agile will not make these applications agile. DevOps and Agile enable us to rethink the complete enterprise architecture of applications.

Recently a CFO was perplexed that every business unit presents that they have cut costs, but their overall margins are still down. Enterprise IT has in its continued effort to focus only on reduction of headcount has been adding technology, but with little or no impact to the overall costs to the organization. Headcount costs are being replaced with technology costs. It is not uncommon for Enterprise IT to be still maintaining an application that may be called once in a decade, but since it is there, they need to maintain it. Automation beyond certain limits may actually lose the cost advantage. To get better return on investment, it may be better for the complete applications to be rearchitected, redesigned and redeveloped.

Many enterprises are facing challenges from start-ups that are more nimble and agile and providing the same services at a fraction of a cost. Many of the established enterprises are finding it challenging to meet the cost structure of these startups due to their inherent cost structure that they manage. The old cost paradigms of people are no longer a differentiator. It is the way they have structured their technology and their ability to adopt to recent technologies that is providing the competitive advantages to these startups. The early paradigm of benefits of scale is also being disproved as the startups seems to be able to provide the same services irrespective of size.

Though the writing on the wall is clear and many Enterprise IT may acknowledge it, and most of business operations demand it, very few enterprises have even attempted to even acknowledge the quagmire that they are currently in due to the legacy applications. As stated earlier, the people who have some knowledge of these legacy applications would start moving out the enterprise over the next decade. Before the last of these people leave the enterprise, Enterprise

IT needs to urgently relook at their enterprise portfolio and metamorphosize for the future by transforming themselves into a butterfly.

A classic example of technology impact in business is in the publishing industry. Both the traditional publishing industry and the new wave of online publishing industry relatively use the same technology. But the difference is on how they use this technology leading to substantial friction between the two. In a tradition industry, most of the books have been computerized and set for printing. But they still print the books in bulk orders and ship them to various bookstores. Also, they need to have substantial demand for books to order a reprint. They have a schedule for printing and a book is slotted as per the calendar of the publishing house. An online publisher can publish the book immediately as soon as the book is uploaded. They have developed tools to convert word processor documents into publishable copies, and letting the author review the format. They provide all the self-help guidelines to enable an author to publish without loss of support of a professional publishing house. If necessary, they provide contact details of other resources, that can support the author in his publication for specific individual tasks at a fraction of the costs as they use global talent pool. Many of these online publishing houses also have a "print on demand" service to enable readers to order a physical copy of the book. This enables an author to publish a book with a few days and in many cases less than a week. Due to this simple change we are now able to read a few hundreds of authors instead of a few that publishing houses used to cater to. There are thousands of unpublished authors who are lost forever due to their books could not pass through the publishing agencies. The reader was restricted to the thoughts of the publishing agencies. The online publishers have unleased thousands of authors and many of these books have a refreshingly new thoughts and ideas with a completely fresh approach to their books.

And as we move forward, even the effort of an author to type a book wills lowly get reduced as voice and brain interfaces take over these tasks. When we write a document or book, there are multiple thoughts in a writer's mind, that they try to place them in their book. But in the process some ideas duly drop off including some initial thoughts that may have been forgotten by the author during typing the document. With voice and brain interfaces these would automatically find a place in the book. When was the last time we saw a teenager actually typing into her mobile? As we move forward, the actual pen-ship of the book may be done by AI programs and only the table of contents and thoughts needs to be provided by the author. The automation tools of the future can structure and lay out the book based on authors thoughts including authoring the complete book!

And as we proceed further, these intelligent programs and augmented reality can scrutinize the book and inform the author of possible readership and suggest price marks for success. They can also reorient the books to enable the author to become successful. Though these tools would be first used by publishers to identify the probability of success of a book and try to use them as proprietary tools internally. These tools may be challenged by one of the publishers or even a startup and provide more user-friendly tools to authors to enable them to make decisions based on analysis that till then was the domain of a publishing house. This would ensure that the complete decision making of a book lifecycle is moved to the author and publishing houses purely become hosts for these authors. Imagine the literature enriched with all the people who have excellent ideas who can put them on paper, the numerous people who are currently confined by language barriers, and the countless people who have a mortal fear of publishing, enriching the world of literature. We are not too far into the future when technology will write, and publish a book purely based on the random thoughts that we can dictate or think during our morning walk!

If publishing industry is one of the early change leaders, other industries are not be far behind. Another industry that would be impacted by on-demand would be manufacturing. Though they have been earlier attempts by automobile industry to manufacture based on specifications of the client, they have floundered. IoT may actually make manufacturing on demand a norm and lead to customer specifications defining the manufacturing process. Already many car owners get customized fits done at the dealers outside the domain of the automobile manufacturer. It may not be long before manufacturers themselves will start providing all these options from their facility. With driverless cars, sensors to track your ability to drive being built inside cars we are moving to a complete transformation of the driving experience. With rapid technology advances, we are not far away from the day when we can completely customize our car based on our requirements.

Defining the future of IT

Enterprise IT needs to first acknowledge that the structure and path of the current IT will no longer be relevant. With more technology savvy business users' who seemingly are far more adept at using technology than any of the previous generations, Enterprise IT need to cater to the future generations of professionals. At the same time Enterprise IT needs to acknowledge the rules of business have transformed over the past couple of decades and will continue to change rapidly. Business evolution would be even more rapid and provide little or no time for internal systems to adapt to the changing business cycles.

Secondly that the Enterprise IT needs to acknowledge is the plethora of technologies that will change the way we use technology daily both at home and office. As Technology and business integrate together, IT needs to be integrated into this environment. The differentiation lines between technology (including IT) and business will evaporate at a faster rate in the future than during the past few decades. And above all, many technologies that start as promising become redundant even before they are commercially launched. Unlike in earlier eras, waiting for the technology leader to emerge before adopting in the enterprise will lead to severe erosion of business value due to rise in competition. The Enterprise inherent procrastination during the initial hype of a technology and awaiting to adopt during the later period or second adapters, may lead to losing competitive advantage.

Thirdly, Enterprise IT needs to acknowledge that way we are currently interfacing with technology, be it using computers or mobiles, itself will undergo dramatic changes as new technologies like gesture recognition, voice recognition, and brain computer interface become available for all users to use for their personal and business environment. Even today most of the keyboard functions have been replaced by voice recognition and fingerprint or facial recognition. Many ATM's of banks have replaced their debit cards with fingerprints and are testing facial recognition. How long before this generation of people who rarely used the keyboard move to workplace and would like to use voice commands for all their work! The NextGen of business and IT professionals would start challenging the gap between business and personal technology space. And most of these technologies may also become redundant if the next wave of computing begins earlier than expected, where programs will write their code and do their own maintenance.

Finally, Enterprise IT needs to acknowledge that legacy will no longer be a few decades old but will be a couple of years old or in some cases even a few months old. This will lead to situation of trying to deliver return of investment immediately instead of over a few years. Many of the ROI calculations of maintenance and major update usually have a 3 to 5-year horizon and any new development have a 5 to 7-year horizon. Enterprise IT needs to junk these outdated ROI models and try to prove their ROI immediately, by enabling enterprises to reduce their costs of business getting reflected within the next couple of quarters and not after a couple of years.

And above all, the consumer may move forward from one technology savvy company to another instead of looking for stable or established company for providing his services. As we observe the young generation their connection with companies that speak to them through technology they appreciate and identify than with established companies. They may interface with a company through technology and never interact with a human being or an employee of the company. And as these generations of people become more dominant in the marketplace most of the established companies will be forced to adapt to the changing dynamics of the marketplace. Consumer loyalty is primarily derived from technology adoption then through life cycle value of customers. As the NextGen is more comfortable interfering with technology, even our traditional definitions of customer loyalty need to be redefined in technology terms. Their fascination with technology will far outweigh the other parameters like longevity, quality etc., They would prefer to adopt an innovative technology tool and be a first adopter than wait. They would like to use the latest technology than use a proven technology and would discard a technology as soon as a newer technology is found.

Planning for the future

With such a rapidly changing scenario and obsolescence always around the corner, Enterprise IT needs to become extremely agile to meet the ever-changing business and technology landscape. To achieve this Enterprise IT needs to completely redefine its role in the Enterprise, and acknowledge that some of the applications and end-user systems are better defined and managed by Business departments than by central Enterprise IT.

To begin this metamorphosis, Enterprise IT needs to dismantle the legacy siloed applications. Especially those that are currently hidden behind the multiple walls of interfaces, integrators, and middleware. Even many of the applications that provide the same functionality from established software vendors have the siloed application architecture at the backend. These are rigid and provide little flexibility. Any enhancement we do will still maintain the primary cost structure and may deliver incremental cost advantages compared to new startups that provide similar consumer experience at a fraction of the cost.

Secondly, Enterprise IT needs to reorganize moving away from legacy thinking to futuristic thinking. They need not worry about how to meet the business requirements with the currently legacy applications or current application portfolio database. Enterprise IT needs to think, what if, the currently application portfolio does not exist, how will they deliver the customer experience.

Thirdly, the enterprise architecture team needs to be proactive in scanning the marketplace for the innovative technologies or applications coming up in the marketplace and define a model to integrate these applications into the Enterprise Application. They should not be hindered by enterprise licensing policies and restrict them to existing technologies and tools. Any architecture should assume that the application they are designing should drastically cut costs with absolutely no legacy applications to be considered.

Fourth, Enterprise IT needs to discuss extensively with the business users on the type of technologies and tools they would like to see, including their view on the future of technology. As business users would be savvier of the latest competition that is providing differentiated services at a fraction of costs, Enterprise IT needs to gather their inputs and ideas. Also encourage the business user to feel that their inputs are highly regarded and appreciated. More often than not, most business users have a low opinion of IT people based on their past experiences. Enterprise IT needs to take the first step and build that bridge.

And finally, Enterprise IT needs to have a health discussion with the business users especially the younger generations and middle management on the future of business applications, and the model of engagement. Many business departments would be glad to take responsibility for their business applications and even adopting third party tools and technologies compared to Enterprises IT. They would cut through the approval process. Have a health discussion on defining a road map for both Enterprise IT and business departments in transitioning the application portfolios to the business. At the same time defining to business users the flexibility that enterprise IT would provide them if they deem it necessary to integrate a third-party tool or technology.

At the same time, Business Departments needs to acknowledge that they have a higher say in the IT than earlier. Instead of complaining about the lack of support from Enterprise IT, they should work with IT for transitioning of the business applications especially the customer facing applications being completely developed and maintained by the business users themselves.

Both the business departments and enterprise IT need to acknowledge that the applications they are discussing have a short life span unlike earlier and may need to be replaced at a short notice. The future will demand new applications being integrated with specific business requirements and may have a shelf life of few months, instead of years and decades.

To achieve this Enterprise IT needs to perform deep introspection and define its role for the future. They need to acknowledge that bloated IT departments, whether in house or outsourced, may not be applicable for the future. The model of the future tacitly admits the "bring your own applications" for the business users and enable them to develop their own applications. Enterprise IT needs to define a world of user enabled applications that may be used for short duration and in a few cases for a few months. These applications may be developed or purchased for a specific business purpose and retired immediately after the business requirement is met. Business users may use different applications to meet the same business requirement with minor or small variations to meet their customer requirements.

As the enterprise IT and business are doing their internal introspection, they need to bring the data science groups into the discussions. More often than not, these data scientists work in isolation away from the businesses and try to identify factors or conditions that impact the business. IT and business need to understand the role of data scientists and work with the data science groups in developing models to equip business users to develop multiple factor models to simulate multiple scenarios based on multiple conditions. The deep insights provided by this group coupled with the business knowledge would provide a competitive advantage. Till either the business users or data scientists do not strive to work together, the analysis and findings will only become a burden to business users with little actual value derived by the users. If the data scientists are working in isolation, it may be more useful to disband them and assign them to business departments. The current model of data science departments working independently of business units may not be sustainable. Business departments already burdened with growing business in a tough environment may support data scientists for a period of time assuming potential deep insights. Unless data scientists start delivering impactful data insights for business growth, they would become another overhead for business users trying to justify the analysis being done by these scientists.

The first option for Enterprise IT Applications is to reorient itself to become the custodian of the enterprise data and a few enterprise applications at the backend. The business department taking the responsibility for business applications and for all customer facing applications. Enterprise IT develops internal application stores that business users can login to build their customizable features based on the enterprise application or to extend the functionality of the enterprise application. As a first step the Enterprise Applications needs to transfer all business application developers to the concerned business department, and the IT developers working closely with the business users. These developers need to embed into the business department directly under the control of the business department and meeting the requirements of the business users. With an IT Savvy business user, the ideas that generated need to be grasped by the IT team and work on ways of meeting those requirements. The Dilbert model of apprehension of business users need to be replaced with a healthy discussion of future of IT. Many of the outlandish thoughts generated by business users needs to be seen in futuristic technology space and defined. The IT team that is transferred to business needs to have a grasp on the recent technologies and trends in technologies. More often than not the new technology trends many not even be in the same industry space.

The second option is for Enterprise IT becoming the custodian of the enterprise data and the complete application portfolio being developed and managed by business departments. Enterprise IT will also be responsible for defining the application integration standards and the compliance requirements along with the enterprise risk management team. Enterprise IT will enable the specific data to be accessed by business departments using their applications. Enterprise IT establishes and becomes the facilitator or tester vis-à-vis the approver of new applications that business would like to download or purchase from the various stores like Play Store, Appstore or AppExchange. Business Departments based on their market and competitor landscape will develop their own applications and if necessary, develop customer specific customizable applications. Business Users may even develop particular use applications to enable the company to win new business. This model promises the maximum flexibility for business users and enable them to react to the rapidly changing market scenarios.

For either of these models to be successful, there needs to be a complete mindset change among enterprise IT, and an openness among the senior management who are more used to Enterprise IT delivering their requirements. Middle and lower business management may be more conducive to these models though with apprehension on trying to figure out the mines in the new path. Though these models are inherently presenting a risky proposal, they can be managed if Enterprises approach with proper planning and execution.

These models will ensure that each enterprise will have its unique business model(s) compared to competition. The uniqueness will stem from the way Enterprise IT integrates the varied applications and Business Departments develop or adapt to the latest tools and technologies in the marketplace to give them their competitive advantage. With hundreds of application tools and technologies propagated within the enterprise, the sheer uniqueness of these combinations and permutations will enable each enterprise to maintain their competitive advantage. *CBInsights* in a series of articles on *Unbundling* the enterprise provides a glimpse into new technologies that can replace the existing IT application portfolio. For the hundreds of options listed in these articles, there are many more alternatives in the marketplace.

The fundamental assumption underlying these two models is the flexibility that they need to provide to business users to adapt new tools and technologies for either adding or replacing the existing tools and technologies. These changes should be in real time and not the months and years that are taken to replace the existing applications.

To begin with Enterprise IT needs to start thinking afresh. Unlike in Year 2000 scenario, where the process started with application portfolio assessment, planning for the future should begin with a complete fresh board. Enterprise IT needs to solicit the future of business by speaking to multiple stake holders that convey the wildest scenarios. Enterprise IT needs to understand the multiple competitive scenarios that are developing in the marketplace, and the timelines that they would see the changes occurring. Enterprises IT and business need to acknowledge that the competitive scenario timeline is changing rapidly and the timeframes for new competition is now in months and not in years to develop the scale of operations to pose a challenge.

Unlike the current trend of sending questionnaires to the enterprise to tabulate results, these surveys should be done at multiple levels, that include questionnaires, focus groups, workshops, interactive meetings and including the vilest requirements gathering model, at the coffee machine. Encourage IT professionals to spend time with business users to encourage a free exchange of ideas and thoughts. Encouraging the interaction should be done over a period of time, and not in a quick bang approach. In the process the chasm of trust deficit that has grown between IT, business users and operations team should develop at least bridges of communication, if not fill the abyss.

At the same time business and IT need to start reviewing the landscape extending their search beyond the traditional competitive landscape to evaluate the future. A few years ago, assuming that a search engine would become a payment gateway was an unforeseen event. Payments were the domain of banking and suddenly banking is seeing independent payment gateways, and multiple online service providers having their own payment gateway. In the process they have completely eroded the charges of payment transfers. In some cases, payment gateways to encourage users have even paid the users, instead of charging them. A few months ago, when we wanted to do an international fund transfer, imagine our surprise when a payment provider charges were less than 10% of bank charges for the same amount. These types of predatory pricing by new payment providers is weaning away the customers from traditional banking services. Similarly, many of the traditional domains of banking is slowly being chipped away by independent online providers with the latest technology including the complete model of international trade, that is being redefined using blockchain. Enterprise IT and business need to look at the new models emerging to reduce their internal costs for payments, trade, and dealer management. Many of the traditional models that have emerged a few decades and continuing with incremental improvements by IT will rapidly undergo complete change in the next few years. Blockchain that emerged with cryptocurrency a few years ago is now rapidly being adapted into multiple areas to reduce transaction costs and improve accuracy. If there was any assumption that blockchain is purely for cryptocurrency, those myths have been busted in the last few years and the technology behind blockchain is being used in multiple industries to provide multiple services including governments.

Confounding the emergence of new business scenarios is the emergence of innovative technology. Innovative technology not just restricted to computers and IT but technology that will change the complete dynamics of business. New technologies that are defining communication like 5G/6G, and new material like graphene, and IoT are slated to revolutionize the ways of our life. How they will change or will impact the consumer is still being discussed, but the impact of these new technologies coupled with emergence of AI, Machine learning, brain computer interface, gesture recognition, and others will transform our lives over the coming years. If the landline took a few decades for people to adopt, mobiles have been lapped up by the people within the shortest feasible time frame. Along with the adoption, all users have kept up with the technology changes that have completely transformed the way we use a mobile over the past decade from a voice based to a data/application-based system. These technology changes have been enabled by rapidly changing data speed protocols that have redefined mobile technology and adoption by the handset providers and eagerly lapped up by the users. From a time when a landline phone was used for multiple years or even decades, the new mobile phones have a shelf life of less than two years in the hands of the consumer. The old adage of "if it ain't broke don't fix it", rarely resonates with the current consumer. It is not uncommon for users to even upgrade their handset the moment it is launched in the market every year. The new adage," if it is new, need to have it," resonates across all the younger generations.

These interactions between business, operations and IT need to be ongoing to ensure that all the stakeholders are together on the future of business. Based on these interactions, the business departments in conjunction with operations and IT need to establish labs within their work areas with latest and emerging technologies. These labs need to be managed jointly and enable business users to spend time in them on their own and play with emerging tech. The users based on their experiences need to define how the technology will enable their customers and provide information about any emerging technology that they have seen in the marketplace. These labs should have a dynamic configuration with new technologies being adapted with quick proof of concepts being developed on a continuous basis to enable users to provide a healthier feedback. These labs should be only for future and emerging tech and work closely with business users than being incubated in some remote corner of the Enterprise IT. In one company the incubation lab was established in a building that was exclusively being used by IT, and all the business users were spread across multiple other buildings. Business users were invited to visit the incubation center periodically for testing and providing feedback. The building was a secure location and only people having access were permitted to enter the building. The moment the secure access was mentioned many of the business users never took the initiative to walk across and work on new technology. And with IT mentioning that access to incubation center was only on invitation, also discouraged other users. When we enquired when the CxO visited, the response was over 18 months, the last business unit head visited over 6 months ago, and a couple of business heads have not visited at all. Unlike these restrictive models of incubation centers, these should be established on working areas for businesses including an incubation center for CxO suite of offices. Executives irrespective of designation should be encouraged to go to the floor and use these new technologies and provide feedback, and suggestions. As these are managed by the business, business users should not only provide feedback, but also suggest methods that would encourage them to develop better business with their customers. Even the CxO's need to continuously spend time with the incubation center and use these new systems to provide them an insight of the future of business, and encourage their teams to continuously review the business landscape, In these new incubation centers, business users should continuously provide feedback about emerging business scenarios and competition, and IT should bring in the pure technology and competitive businesses model live in the incubation center. Jointly they need to provide scenarios, what-if analysis, with live models to encourage users to experience the future, without restrictive times, or scheduled invitations. The business users should have a flexibility to visit and observe, even at off hours when the center itself may not have any person available to clarify any doubts to encourage unassisted experiences. Also, irrespective of the business departments, other business users should also be encouraged to visit the other incubation centers and provide feedback. The business users should be encouraged to visit the center multiple times to experience the new wave of technologies.

Creating the New Architecture

After intensive interactions with business users, IT should rearchitect it models of the future (MOF). The MOF should be a working document with the team meeting frequently and adding new members to keep updating the new technologies and business imperatives.

One of the biggest challenges today is the shackles for the architecture team that is hindered by the legacy applications that restrict the innovation or curb the thinking process. The moment enterprise architecture is mentioned they list an enormous number of hinderances and why it is not possible. More than actual technological hindrances the biggest speed bump has been the lower than expected results promised by IT over the past few years or the time they have taken to implement a new solution. Enterprise IT has thrown multiple phrases like Digital Transformation, Online transformation, Application Transformation etc., and have rarely been successfully delivered or when delivered completely befuddled the business users. Above these hinderances, most of the business users and operations perceive IT more of tool for cost reduction and operational efficiency than actual business enabling tool. Tragically the moment cost reduction crops up the headcount reduction rears its ugly head.

The other biggest challenge is the language barriers between technology and business teams. It is not uncommon for us to sit in meetings where the IT is presenting it solutions in technical terms and business users are completely clueless on the impact of the solution on its operations. The common cliched terms of time to market, cost reduction etc., have been overused by IT teams that the moment they are uttered they lose the business users. A few years ago, I was invited for evaluation of CRM tools by our company. The vendor started the presentation by speaking about the architecture and various modules. About half-an-hour into the presentation, I raised my hand for a question and was informed that all questions would be taken at the end, and they confidently informed me that most of the questions that I may have would be answered during the course of the presentation. For the next three hours the vendor team consisting of about a dozen specialists droned on about the superiority of their technology and how their architecture will provide the competitive advantage. After the three and half hour's presentation, and after they completed their presentation, I again raised my hand and requested them to show me how their CRM will function from account creation, to opportunity creation to closure. The room went absolutely silent, and then all confusion reigned. They came back and said that they will schedule a separate meeting with the other team that can walk us through the opportunity lifecycle. We returned to our office and imagine the amusement my colleagues had at my expense after that.

The third challenge is as IT department started focusing only on individual department, more often than not, they have forgotten the enterprise impact of their solutions. In an instance when IT was provided the challenge of reducing invoices to finance department, they signed with a third-party who will consolidate the enterprise vendors invoices and submit one consolidated invoice to the company, and the company will pay the third-party and the third-party will pay the vendors. In the process, Finance slashed its processing of number of invoices drastically. But the challenge started immediately after implementation. The third-party did not have XML interface for vendors to upload their invoices, and all invoices have to be manually entered into the third-party portal. The third-party used to consolidate all invoices in a two-week period and submit the invoices to the customer. After a couple of months, the individual divisions within the company started having challenges in reconciling the invoices to their internal divisions. In the process, IT has created other issues to solve one problem.

The MOF should consider all interfaces and interactions to come out with a clear baseline on how each application will impact all the concerned departments. The MOF should also clearly outline the risk and challenges clearly in business terms. This can only be achieved if business users become part of the Enterprise Architecture Definition teams and play an active role while defining the MOF. The business users in MOF Definition team should also become the champions for propagating the new architecture model to other business users and encourage inputs from various business users. The MOF should be continuously discussed, and all updates provided to business users soliciting their inputs. The business users should feel that they can look to IT not just for cost reduction and operational efficiency but to enable them to grow their business and get new business. The business users should own the enterprise IT architecture as a business growth engine.

Enterprise IT should encourage active discussions on their plans and solicit new technologies and business changes continuously from business. To achieve this enterprise IT departments should clearly state their goals in business language and not speak about modules and technologies. For most of the business users they are least worried whether the application is developed in COBOL, Java, or Python and are even less concerned whether waterfall, spiral, agile or devops models are used. They are more concerned about the look and feel, and how they will interact with the system and the time it will take to onboard a new customer. It is not uncommon for the same customer or vendor to submit the same set of documents into multiple divisions of enterprise to start working with that division. Customer or vendor registered with one division rarely becomes the customer o vendor for another division. IT could have enabled this process, but in most of the enterprise has not done so. Using blockchain this process can be simplified, and only additional information can be solicited. I was interacting with a business user, and I asked him why he does not let his customers use the computer interface instead of his trying to fill the application on their behalf. The look of horror on the business user was palpable. He answered that there is no way he will ever let a customer see the user interface as he considered the look and feel as atrocious and the form was completely confusing. When I enquired why he did not give the feedback to IT, he said he had done so, and received a response that it is in the change request queue and one of the IT GUI specialists would contact him to take his requirements and that was over a quarter ago. The business user was confident that if the GUI specialist contacts him in the next six months and they implement within a year he will be happy. Even a small request that he had made is still to be implemented. In the application he was discussing, the application has a start date, duration, and an end date, all to be filled manually by the user. He has requested the IT to automate the process to define the end date based on the duration of the contract from the start date. That is also pending for IT person to meet him to discuss the change requirement. The IT teams' response was that business users were always causing issues and most of them are trivial and they have done the look and feel based on the corporate standards, and the start date-duration-end date issue was based on the requirements definition document that was signed off by the business users.

Though both the viewpoints from a process point of view are correct and they have evidence for an audit trail. Tragically both are WRONG. The primary purpose of the applications was to enable customers provide the information on their own. The secondary purpose was to reduce the errors while filling up the application. The primary purpose was lost as none of the business users were exposing the application to customers as they feel the user interfaces is confusing and audacious. The secondary purpose was lost as any mathematical calculations would lead to error, without clear error message or automated wherever possible. Though the fault may partially lie with the business users the primary responsibility should lie with the enterprise IT. How many applications or presentations do we see with blue color, simply because the corporate color scheme defines blue as their color scheme. In the 16 million colors available we are reduced to small spectrum of various shades of blue. It is also high time IT acknowledges the fact that very few quantitative science people have great artistic skills and they need to ensure that user interfaces are designed by people with an artistic skill and not with quantitative skills.

When enterprise IT is presenting the MOF, it should strive to get a complete buy in from the business users and address their concerns and points and how they will be managed. It is quite common for pushing contentious points into point 45 of 50-point presentation where the time spent on the contentious point would be a passing glance, and both business and IT have a completely different understanding. IT assuming it as approved and business assuming it is yet to be discussed. The better approach is discussing the contentious points ahead, develop multiple champions among business users and leverage them to respond to concerns from other users. At the same time, IT should be flexible enough to change its' position if the suggestion made by a business user make logical or business sense. Instead of waiting for a future scenario that may hit us, it is better understood and addressed earlier. This is also imperative that Enterprise IT understands the requirements more accurately and discuss with business users on their requirements and find ways to bridge the gap. It is not uncommon for us to see CRM systems heavily customized to meet the requirements of production and finance system to the chagrin of salespeople who more often than not abandon using the CRM system. Similarly, production and finance systems replicate the data from CRM or from the other departments that they have little or no clue why they need to input the data. As these systems rarely speak to each other, most of the data is duplicated or triplicated and has to be manually entered. Enterprise IT needs to keep asking critical questions on why a suggestion from another department is required in the systems of another department. Also, if the data flow can be designed to ensure that manual entry of data or validation is minimized. These cross pollination of required information from one department into another has led to current IT Systems becoming a bane instead of useful tool for productivity enhancements. Many cross validations that can be done by using the system are manually done.

The common refrain is that due to risk and compliance regulations they cannot automate the system. If required MOF may need to redefine the complete risk and compliance framework for the enterprise. In many enterprises it is not uncommon for multiple versions of risk and compliance regulations co-existing that span the business environment of a few decades. These need to be critically evaluated and redefined for the MOF from the current state of risk and compliance. Enterprise risk and compliance frameworks would be constantly challenged and violated unless the risk and compliance framework keep itself up to date with changing business environment.

The MOF should be able to meet the business requirements in a few days or weeks not in months or years. If required they should be able to make a complete turn based on changing business scenarios. Though this may lead to chaos in the beginning, the MOF should be able to bring order from Chaos. The only constant in the MOF would be chaos. While defining the MOF, it is advisable if the current applications are discussed more from each process point of view and solicit the best in class including from other industries. Instead of discussing about CRM, the discussions should be more at customer onboarding, customer offboarding and multiple layers of customer management. Similarly, instead of discussing at a payment application level, it may be subdivided into multiple layers of person-to-person, person-to-enterprise, vendors to enterprise, enterprise to customers, and every other scenario possible. For each of these scenarios look to the marketplace to identify the leading providers and at what rate they are providing the services and benchmark to provide similar services. Also define the what-if scenarios, of these alternative companies moving into business landscape. The biggest advantage businesses can bring to the MOF is to bring the emerging technology landscape and creating multiple scenarios on how they will impact their future business.

Finally, this model should evolve from within the organization as you define the MOF to ensure that your organization maintains its competitive advantage, and IT provides that business flexibility. Consultant organizations may present to you, but only use them for information and ideas, but every point of reference made by the consultant should be discussed and seen for its adaptability inside the MOF. Also be aware that cut and paste features and knowledge databases have replaced originality and it is not uncommon that many of the solutions, designs and architectures are primarily cut and paste with little or no modification from other earlier solutions. The use of cut and paste has increased the number of consultants but fewer original thinkers. It is not uncommon for many vendors to have consulting divisions who would provide you the frameworks with an inherent assumption to get future business, but most of these are limited to the solutions provided by the vendor and in many cases they attempt to force-fit or extend the solution architecture beyond the extremes of the solution. If there are any vendors providing you on latest technologies do request them to present their MOF ideas to you to enable you to consider, evaluate and adopt the relevant to your enterprise's MOF. And let us accept that the buck starts and stops with the Enterprise IT Department.

The challenges with Legacy

The biggest challenge for many Enterprise IT Architects and CIO's is the legacy applications that are the lifeline of the enterprise. These applications contain decades of knowledge and functionality. They form the core of the enterprise transactions. Many Enterprise IT are even scared to imagine a life without these applications. It is time they are retired with respect!

Every Industry needs that moment of reckoning. Enterprise IT's moment of reckoning is just around the corner. It is time the challenge is taken head-on and tackled by it horns. Though the first timers five to six decades ago never had the challenges and dependence an enterprise has on IT, and they slowly evolved to current scenario.

The good news is that though the moment of reckoning has come, we can still do a gradual metamorphosis of the complete enterprise IT. Enterprise IT needs to acknowledge that the applications or the platform on which they run do not provide the competitive advantage. With dead code, unused code and multiple layers of middleware, these applications have ceased to provide the competitive advantage. But the knowledge, functional and data-driven, provide the real advantage, and if they are harnessed optimally, Enterprise IT can again provide the competitive advantage that business is anticipating from IT. Though the CTO divisions have successfully transitioned or in the process of transition, the applications under the CIO need to transition for the MOF.

To begin with acknowledge the challenges and limitations of current IT applications portfolio and the team skill dependency. Most of the enterprises if they commence their metamorphosis to the MOF will be able to complete the transition in a gradual manner with minimal impact on their annual budget. But to do it this CIO's need have a discussion with the CxO's that there will be no cost efficiency in IT Departments and may need additional budget for the next few years.

The first step would be to identify the complete application portfolio at the enterprise and department levels and their usage within the organization including the business departments that access these applications. There are enough enterprise application assessor tools that can be used to perform the enterprise applications assessments. The biggest challenge would be availability of people who have the intricate knowledge of the applications. This may require collaboration with CTO department and require his resources to enable the complete inventory of applications are properly collaborated.

The inventory of the application portfolio should include a comprehensive information of

- the complete application portfolio at the enterprise and department levels
- Logical data flow diagrams
- the data interfaces and interactions among the applications
- The languages and versions
- Application packages, third-party products, versions, availability of source code, and availability of vendor

- Availability of source code, lines of source code (with and without comments)
- Dead, unused and rarely used applications
- documentation for the applications
- Packages, source code and the availability of package vendors
- Functional specifications
- Detailed design documents

It would not be a surprise that enterprises to varying percentages will have applications with no source code, no documentation, no design documents, and no functional specifications. It will also be no surprise that while drawing the data flow diagrams there will be programs that the data will call during its processing but have absolutely no functional knowledge. There may even be programs that have never been used as the code was written to handle exceptions and that exceptional situation has not arisen in the past few years. There yet may be some programs that may have been purchased and the vendors have long been out of business or have been acquired multiple times with no person in the enterprise having a clue on support related queries. Even Enterprises that implemented ERP and other application packages have done extensive modifications and customizations that have little resemblance to the original package and any upgrade is as expensive, both cost and effort wise. It is also not uncommon for enterprises to have multiple versions of the same application package running in different divisions or locations. It is also not uncommon for enterprises to have multiple application packages performing exactly the same functionality and used for exactly the same operations.

Though this may seem to simple tool-based assessment, the actual assessment will be a nightmare for the team performing the assessment. One way is to start with the data flow using sample test cases that involve common fields like data name or transaction value. But as they keep reviewing their application portfolio and they would be surprised to see the number of applications that have not been updated by the previous generations. This assessment many have to done also using the inventory from the CTO teams to support in locating all the missing application programs. Though many companies did perform an enterprise portfolio analysis during the Year 2000 project days, most of these have not been updated. But if the enterprise portfolio analysis documents from year 2000 project days do exist, they may be a good place to start.

In parallel, the business units and operations teams need to perform a process level analysis and map all the processes followed within the department, and that involve multiple departments. The standard operating procedures needs to be validated for accuracy and updated with the latest information.

It would not be a surprise as Enterprises would realize the number of applications or process documentation that have not been updated as the enterprises pushed for higher and higher operational efficiency. After both the departments, the Enterprise IT and Business/Operations team have created an acceptable level of documentation, both the teams need to meet and starting cross mapping the two documents. For every process step that is being defined by the business and operations team, IT needs to identify the applications involved. Though this looks like a logical step, the two teams usually speak two different languages with neither understanding the other, nor ensuring that the two teams could actually speak the common language is like finding the philosophers' stone. After the two teams cross-map their processes and applications at the elemental level, the teams should review the unused or dead processes and applications for usage in the future. At the same time, both the teams need to critically review the duplication of data solicitation, transactional processing across multiple processes and applications. They need to review if they can be consolidated and make a real improvement that impact both applications and processes.

Any process improvement involves technology intervention and needs to surmount the rules of risk and compliance. More often than not, process improvement is defined based on internal benchmarking, improving year on year. After the cross-mapping is done, the teams need to have a healthy discussion with Risk and compliance to review the applicability of the rules for the future and retire any archaic rules. The team may have to review and present how the new startup is able to meet the compliance requirements at a fraction of costs and critically evaluate what they need to evaluate to meet the requirements of the future. The benefit of established enterprise is the presence of customer base and can start immediately with a higher number of transactions compared to a startup. Companies need to leverage the economies of scale and critically look at reducing costs and not be wound up internally with process and compliance.

Managing the complexity

The metamorphosis of the enterprise IT would be the most complex project any IT Department can undertake. This would involve constantly changing business requirements and technology landscape. Unlike in the past, where the requirements were frozen and signed off, the MOF would involve constantly changing the scope and, in some instances, making a rapid turn to take advantage of any new technology or new business model.

In this complex scenario, enterprises that have relied heavily on vendors would be hard pressed to define a working model for the future and may invariably rely on the traditional time and material models or a variation there of. Even today, it is not uncommon for vendors to try to force-fit elements of waterfall model into any developmental activity and dilute the essential aspects of new developmental models. This model with vendors would inevitably lead to chaos and cost overruns and the current set of vendors will be restricted by the skill set of their internal team. Teams working in new technologies would be limited and may be restricted to their internal research. Evaluating a vendor's skill by the presentations by a few or interacting with a few team members may not provide the true DNA of the vendor.

The Model of the Future requires complete flexibility and ability to adapt the latest technology with little or no resistance and enable the enterprise to move forward. This inherent assumption itself would put restrictions on vendors capability to deliver. More often than not, most of us look to established companies for tools and technologies, including products. The challenge with most of these products and third-party applications are their origins belong to a bygone era and these applications have been web enabled or mobile enabled but rarely or never been rewritten. Many of these products and third-party applications that started in megabytes in both memory and storage today have ballooned to gigabytes in both memory and storage. Most of the additional features are rarely used in a corporate environment, but they will inherit it as vendors try to sell the full suite and not the required components of their application package.

The need is to manage the complex levers that are constantly moving and controlling them. As each business strives to develop its own DNA in response to the changing business landscape, it will be the responsibility of the enterprise IT to ensure that the fruits do not fall far from the tree. The business should have unfettered flexibility to adapt to the changing landscape, and at the same time the responsibility for tracking the changes being made and its impact on other business units and the enterprise remains with the Enterprise IT Team. The fundamental role of Enterprise IT would move from development to become the conductor of the symphony, playing fusion music, with one vital difference the musicians keep changing during the performance and the conductor is expected to still provide the frisson without missing a single note of the music.

To orchestrate such a complex changeover of enterprise IT, the project and portfolio management needs to be expanded to include both IT and business users. This would be a complex maze of third-party solutions for specific functionality and in-house integration of these components.

For every legacy application that would be replaced, Enterprise IT and business users need to critically evaluate if the complete functionality residing in the system is still required for the future, and if the some of the common functionality can be called out from a different application and reduce duplication of functionality. Similarly, where there are multiple applications providing the same functionality, if the requirements can be combined so that it does not become a huge behemoth and potpourri of all departments requirements to become unusable. In many of the cases, most of the information collected by the system has evolved and many fields are there for historical reasons than for any particular use. Any question usually solicits a response that it has been there even before we joined the company decades ago. Some of these may just have been a carry forward from the paper era, when they used some fields for departmental identification and has no value today. All such functionalities need to be clearly called out and removed.

Even when replacing with application packages review for vendors who can provide the functionality required and not the whole suite and activate only the specific licenses. Your systems will still need additional memory and space. Every additional module sitting your system that is unused only leads to confusion and management issues. As an example, when you implement a CRM Solution, most of the CRM vendors provide the package with components of procurement and finance that you will never use as most enterprises have other packages for procurement and finance. But the application that will be installed on your system will include these components as well, and only the CRM part is activated as per your license. It is also not uncommon for vendors to add a lot of extensions in the installed application, that resides on your system with doing absolutely nothing except that that vendor has a policy to activate those components based on license. All these unused, unlicensed components only add to the confusion or restrict the flexibility of enterprise in reducing the costs.

The new wave of competition has broken down every department into its component level. For example, a payments provider now has multiple specializations with multiple vendors providing a specific payment service, each of these have a specific functionality and each of these service providers are providing these services at a fraction of the cost compared to traditional payment providers. Many of these vendors are slowly replacing credit cards and cash for payments. Many of the traditional providers are still charging a high fee for payments when there are cheaper alternatives in the marketplace. It is this granularity that Project and Portfolio Management Team needs to dive into and at the same time provide flexibility to replace any of these components with an alternative when an even cheaper, faster and better alternative becomes available in a complete new technology or may become completely automated.

Attempting such a momentous change would challenge the complete fabric of the enterprise. Every enterprise needs to evaluate the time frame they have to move to the MOF. Based on their dependence of legacy applications, availability of skills, and business landscape change patterns, every enterprise needs to draw its roadmap for the changes. Though we may start with an optimal time span, we need to be prepared for sudden business scenarios and move the schedules around to meet the business requirements. With every delivered change, Enterprise IT needs to be able to provide that they are ahead of the market curve and completely aligned with the business requirements. The decades old perceptions chasm between Enterprise IT and business users need to be bridged with every step of the change implementation. Enterprise IT need to destroy all the broken promises over the decades when the expectations were raised high but due to established programs the delivered results were lower, especially the promises left unfulfilled during the web transformation, online transformation, digital transformation, and mobile transformation. Enterprise IT has used large words with innumerable abbreviations raising the expectations, with little or no palpable changes in the actual business scenario.

Begin with a process map that has been completely mapped with IT Applications that has the maximum impact on business users and that would need replacement on a priority due to multiple reasons like vendor not available, fragmented business process embedded into the application, source code not available or for the simple reason that it is completely standalone. Redevelop the application by taking the functional knowledge from the application, but completely redevelop by removing all the dead and unused functionality, duplicate information that can referenced from other applications, and using latest technologies like blockchain, inbuilt AI, machine learning voice recognition, gesture recognition, and inbuilt relevant data analytics etc., to completely redefine the application-business user interface. Though the middle and senior management may have challenges, wow the young managers, and people who actually use the application. The application should be open to allow business users to plug and play third-party add-ins and perform their own data analysis and reports.

At the same time, the business users need to be clear of the flexibility of the MOF by demonstrating to users on freedom to change the new applications with third-party tools and ease of use. Enterprise IT needs to demonstrate the improvement in applications, and reporting over a period of time using the AI and data analytics tools developed or installed with the application.

As Enterprises have a period of time, they can plan their activities for complete metamorphosis of the applications beginning with legacy application dependent processes and slowly move outward to the processes that have been recently updated with new applications or technologies. The key component of building the plan is to ensure that there may be a major change that would require the managers to redesign their complete plan. It is imperative that enterprise IT gets unshackled from legacy applications and start using the latest technology for business competitiveness.

With over 65000 startups and more getting added every year catering to data, AI, voice recognition, gesture recognition, machine learning, fintech, insuretech, retailtech, etc., the enterprise applications will see a major change from the current application landscape. Besides this even established software vendors are opening application stores that enables thousands of users to upload their developed applications, the dependence of application coding would slowly be replaced by application gluing. Application development and maintenance would be replaced by a completely new paradigm of Application Management, that would involve adding, gluing, and retiring the applications in real time. Many of the add-on modules that used to be custom developed are now available on these application stores reducing the application development cycle from a few months and years to a few days by just gluing in the application from the store. (I am purposefully not using the word integration as this word has been used liberally that it has become too generic to even discuss it. When we mean gluing, we mean an application will be added without modifications to logic, and may require only some snipping like variable changes to be added to existing application portfolio, and as glued paper can be removed carefully, the applications can also be removed and a new application added with minimal effort but carefully). Glue usually wears off, ensuring that an existing application needs to be replaced.

When working with startups, enterprises need to go beyond the investor mindset. Venture capitalists, investors, and angel investors primarily look for both technology and management that would provide them the high rate of returns over a period of time. But enterprises need to look at startups from providing the competitive advantage. Some startup management teams may not be successful be successful in their pitches to investors but may have an excellent product that would provide you that niche advantage over others. Enterprises should solicit such kind of startups as their return on investment is not from the startup but their inherent ability to glue the technology and application from the startup into their MOF.

Though many managers would accept that their application portfolio needs a compete refresh they rarely attempt it. One of the biggest challenges is with the new technology providers and startups. These companies are high on passion and technology but with little or no practical project management principles of delivering to time or schedules and in some cases testing in real life scenarios. It is quite common to come out with an idealistic architecture by the startups but the moment they are put in production either these applications become burdensome for the amount of information asked or the results provided with a far cry from the originally stated benchmarks. The best illustration is the location finding services on a mobile, every mobile application request for it, even if the application has nothing to do with location in foggiest way possible. These companies have a challenge in working with enterprises. Many of these startups have an upstart mentality, and either they disdain the enterprises or at the other end of the spectrum and accept all changes or requests from the enterprise IT. It is the responsibility of the MOF Implementation teams to either prod or cool their belligerence and have real expectations for implementing solutions from these start-ups. As an early mover or first-adopter to any innovative technology enterprises can negotiate better rewards from these enterprises. But being an early mover will also raise the risk for an enterprise in the eventuality that the startup flounders on its path due to financial or other challenges. MOF Implementation teams need to create a risk mitigation plan during the contractual phase with the startup or always have alternative vendors identified for replacement. Once the solution from a startup has been implemented they need to be completely monitored to see if they are continuing to maintain the technology and cost advantage, or their solution is adding layers without the necessary changes to application to maintain the advantage, or if any competitor has emerged that will provide the competitive advantage in technology and cost.

One of the biggest challenges that MOF Implementation team needs to surmount is, if there are multiple application failures occurring simultaneously. Harvard Business Review *(The Tragic Crash of*

Flight AF447 Shows the Unlikely but Catastrophic Consequences of Automation, Sept 2017), discusses the challenges of multiple points of failure in a highly automated system. Though automation has enormous advantages, the article also illustrates the dangers of automation, and our reliance on automation than on manual capabilities. In the current system, with unknown applications chugging along, or in future with heavily automated systems, the impact of multiple system failure will have adversarial effect on the business. The old adage, if it ain't broke don't fix it, may not be applicable as any break that will occur will have catastrophic consequences. Though Enterprise IT may not directly impact the lives of people, it will indirectly have a far larger impact on the livelihood of far greater number of people. To manage such a type of situations the Enterprises IT Team needs to maintain a key team that can manage any type of eventuality, especially that would impact multiple business units and across the enterprise. The team should have dedicated program managers who can immediately move resources to isolate the problem and contain the impact of these multisystem failures. If required, the team should be able to hot-swap or short-circuit some of the applications on a priority basis with minimal impact to the business.

As we look back into the last five decades many companies that were at their zenith have lagged behind due to technology changes. The next few decades will continue to see the turmoil in the marketplace as new companies using better technology will challenge the established companies, and in the process overtake them. Many companies that were considered unassailable have been either acquired or merged or simply have gone out of business. Unless we can learn management lessons from historical fallacies and keep ourselves abreast of the future technology and competition, we will continue to see the turmoil to continue. The churn in the ocean will continue to throw new and brighter ideas emerging as companies leading to a complete transformation in the way we do business and change our lives. As I type this book, I do not foresee the future generation writers will spend their time typing out thousands of words, but may dictate the words and let an application do the translation to words, sentences, paragraphs, and chapters including checking for grammar, syntax and style and push it for printing.

www.ingramcontent.com/pod-product-compliance
Lightning Source LLC
Chambersburg PA
CBHW021824170526
45157CB00007B/2675